The

WORD
EFFECT

The WORD EFFECT

7 Simple Words to
Create Your Most Beautiful Life

by

BECKY JANE KEMP

www.becomingwithbecky.com

LEADERSHIP

Thoughtful. Relevant Leaders From Around The World

BOOKS

Published by Leadership Books, Inc.
Las Vegas, NV – New York, NY

LeadershipBooks.com

ISBN:
978-1-951648-60-2 (Hardcover)
978-1-951648-61-9 (Paperback)
978-1-951648-62-6 (eBook)

ACKNOWLEDGMENTS

This idea would not have happened without the amazing connection of others who have gifts that have helped me take an idea from my heart and move it forward. As I began to acknowledge my dreams and desires out loud, the people, resources, and opportunities presented themselves to make this dream of writing a book a reality.

A special thanks to Suzanne Kimball-Rekow for helping me get this message of light and truth out and editing the thoughts that were put in my heart.

DEDICATIONS

Even though I know there will be several more times throughout my life when I will find myself saying, "This is not the plan," I am grateful that, with the power of words, I can be reminded of the simple truth to focus on the solutions instead of the obstacles.

A special thanks goes first to God for putting this simple truth in my heart and for the courage and capacity to share it with others. Next to my amazing husband, Kris, and my five incredible boys, Kayden, Tyler, Jarret, Trevor, and Jack, who each allow me to continue trying to become my most beautiful self.

FORWARD

Illuminating the obvious. Consider that for a moment.

Many of the processes going on in our mind are in this space - obvious once brought to our attention, but completely unnoticed up until that point.

Like the feeling of your clothes... Can you feel them?

Well, *NOW* you can feel your clothes since I brought them to your attention - but that tactile sensation was completely unnoticed to you until I mentioned it.

Or the fact that you are now reading this foreword in English. Did you notice? It's obvious now that I call it to your attention, but you were oblivious to it right up until the time I so skillfully pointed it out.

I met Becky Kemp at a meeting for the National Speaker's Association where she had the privilege of the platform. Her poise and confidence caught my attention as she began to illuminate the obvious to her professional speaking colleagues.

I hadn't heard Becky speak before, and up until that time I didn't even know she was a member of our chapter. There are many aspiring speakers that come to our meetings, but this one had done her homework. Some speakers tout trite, fluffy platitudes that we too-often hear from the stage. Becky was bringing it with power, referencing time-proven principles of positive psychology I spent over three decades to acquire as a professional psychologist. She captured my attention with the breadth of her reading and experience, including quotations from some of the masters who had been on my podcast mic like Kevin Hall, Craig Manning, and Chad Hymas.

What Becky illuminates through her work is the power of words. I've learned through my professional experience that words are marching orders for the mind. As if our mind is patiently, dutifully waiting for words so it will know which direction to go.

When we say, "I don't think I can do this," our mind gives a crisp salute and responds with "Aye aye Captain!"

When we ask, "How can I do this?" our mind scrambles to action with "I'm on it Captain!"

A lot of folks don't realize our brain has two main jobs: To keep us safe, and to prove us right. This is important because these two objectives help keep us alive and in the game. Unfortunately, both of these brain tasks also get us into trouble We have to use caution in operating the equipment!

Pay attention as Becky illuminates the obvious through *The Word Effect*. Not only will you get powerful mental tools solidly grounded in proven psychological principles, but she also shares a very authentic personal perspective with practical applications. Becky has synthesized in *The Word Effect* what every personal development guru has been trying to teach us... That to experience a more full and abundant life you don't have to change a *THING* - you simply need to change a *THINK*. We do that through carefully selecting our words.

Paul H. Jenkins, Ph.D.
Positivity Psychologist, Author, Speaker
https://DrPaulJenkins.com

Becky Kemp has synthesized in *The Word Effect* what every personal development guru has been trying to teach us… That to experience a more full and abundant life you don't have to change a THING - you simply need to change a THINK. We do that through carefully selecting our words.

Paul H. Jenkins, Ph.D.
Positivity Psychologist, Author, Speaker
https://DrPaulJenkins.com

How I loved your book! I believe you will help many in your path with your vulnerability and insight. There are so many gold nuggets of truth and encouragement in your manuscript.

Let me know when your book is available. I would be happy to offer an endorsement and share on my social media.

Here is a quote you can use from me. Feel free to make edits or changes and let me know if you prefer something different!

"Becky gives us simple tools to rise up with positivity and confidence to conquer life's challenges one word at a time. Her method lifts us out of negative self-talk and teaches us how to find true joy."

Heidi Tucker
Award-winning author and speaker

"Who knew how powerful 7 simple words could be? "The Word Effect" shows us how deeply our inner thoughts and desires are connected to the words we use. Becky teaches that we empower ourselves and others when we intentionally choose words that inspire positive actions."

Ellie Bodily, MSN, RN

Thank you so much for allowing me to be one of the people that you trust and believe in for this opportunity.

Great JOB! So well done! Your book is Fantastic! It will change many lives!

Here is my endorsement. You are welcome to have your editor make slight changes as needed.

We all know that "Our Words Matter", this is not a new concept. Yet, when you read and implement the 7 profound words and the process that Becky has built into this book, you are able to achieve levels beyond what you ever thought possible. As you change as a person, your influence and impact increases, which allows you to transform not only your own life but the lives of others. Embrace the teachings in this book and watch as you soar in confidence and success.

~Kris Barney, CEO All Things Possible, Inc. Author of "Leadership from the Inside Out – Are You the Leader YOU Would Follow?

Kris Barney
Past President-NSA Mtn West 2020-2021
CEO-All Things Possible, Inc.
www.KrisBarney.com

ENDORSEMENT FOR BECKY KEMP "THE WORD EFFECT"

We all struggle in areas of our lives and just want to have Joy, Abundance, and all that is good. The stories written in The Word Effect by Becky Kemp are very relatable. The seven simple steps to along with workbook sheets are a bonus feature for understanding how to make our words matter. Because they do!

- Aida Woodward, Holistic Health Coach

"Becky's personal stories make her principles come alive in a way that is both relatable and crystal clear. *Words Matter* is a powerful read that reminds us how words can impact the human spirit. I have recommitted myself to use my words as a way to positively influence and enhance my own quality of life."

-Julie Lee, Keynote speaker, Author of *I See You; How Compassion and Connection Save Lives*

When it comes to giving you a powerful tool to transform your negative mindset into an empowering mindset, Becky Kemp is a genius! I could completely relate to her vulnerable, inspiring story. Her real-life examples showed me how, step by step, to apply the use of her seven powerful words to my own life to create more peace within, a deeper connection to God, and the courage to pursue my dreams. If you have FOMO (Fear Of Missing Out) you will want to read The Word Effect, 7 Simple Words To Create Your Most Beautiful Life.

–Janette VanLeer, Author of the Transformation Code,
and trainer for Transformation Coaches and Energy Practitioners

Words matter, and nobody shares this with more passion and power than Becky Kemp. Her research and life experiences anchor these life shifting truths—"change your words, change your life." A must-read!

Connie Sokol,
Bestselling author, speaker, TV contributor,
founder Disciple Thought Leaders

TABLE OF CONTENTS

INTRODUCTION

THE EXTRAORDINARY POWER OF WORDS

---

*"One word could change the world for the better.
Words are like passwords.
They unlock the power. They open the door."*
—Kevin Hall

In the beginning of 2005, I lay on an ultrasound table looking anxiously at the technician who was about to perform an imaging test to reveal the gender of my baby. This would be child number four for me and my husband, Kris, who held my hand as the tech took all the typical measurements and ran through a series of tests that generally happen around the twentieth week of pregnancy. As she finished up, she asked if we were ready to hear the sex of the baby. I looked at my husband, squeezed his hand a bit tighter, and gave an affirmative nod.

I had some big expectations that day, to say the least. I was confident that this time, finally, we were going to hear the words *baby girl*. At least, that was what I was hoping would come out of the tech's mouth. It had to be a girl, right? I had already given birth to three boys, and the odds must surely be in my favor: This time, I would get to have the daughter I had been dreaming of my entire life. Then the technician smiled and said, "Congratulations, you have a healthy baby boy coming!"

Boooooooyyyy! The word seemed to come out of her mouth in slow motion, the warped, distorted sound crashing into my ears with force. Instantly my heart sank! I didn't even hear the word *healthy* because I was so fixated on *boy*.

The tech could see the look on my face and quickly excused herself. Tears began to fall. I was embarrassed to be crying—of course, I knew there were women out there who desperately wanted a baby, yet here I was, tearing up because this would be boy number four. I knew I "should be" happy and certainly more grateful. But at that moment, my secret desire of having a daughter was out of reach, out of my control. That thought devastated me.

My sweet and loving husband looked at me, a bit confused, and asked as kindly as he knew how, "Becky, why are you crying? We were just told the baby is healthy and all is going well with the pregnancy."

I sheepishly smiled, wiped my tears, and said, "I know, and I'm so grateful he's healthy. Just give me a minute. If someone had just told you this was going to be your fourth girl, you might be crying too."

As I look back on that experience, I am amazed at the power of one word! One little word brought up different emotions for me than it did for my husband. While he was happily thinking, "Whew! I won't have to sit through any dance recitals," I was feeling miserable. I thought about all the things I would miss, like dressing my little girl in cute clothes with ribbons and bows, sending her on her first date, helping her buy a prom dress, and planning her wedding. I was even thinking about how much I would love attending those dance recitals!

Regardless of how each of us felt when we heard the word *boy*, the fact was Kris and I were having another son. This was our circumstance, but the word itself was not what created the feelings each of us was having about that circumstance. Rather, the *thoughts* we attached to our circumstances determined our feelings. The thoughts I had about what I presumed I would miss out on by not having a girl were what caused my sad and tearful reaction.

Brooke Castillo, a master certified life coach, has said, "Facts don't hurt. The circumstances of our lives have no effect on us until they encounter the mind and we attach meaning to them." This is true: Facts don't have an effect on us. It's what we think (using words we associate with those facts) that causes us to feel certain ways.

My experience that day (and so many other experiences I have had since) with the power my thoughts and feelings had over me regarding one little word has led me to a life-changing realization . . .

Words Matter!
They have the power to shape our thoughts and therefore
our reality, which ultimately determines what kind of
life we create.

The idea that words matter and have the potential to transform us, either for good or bad, is what I lovingly call the **Word Effect**. It has become a principle of great power in my life—one that has awakened me to new ways of looking at things, shifted my thinking away from negativity and given me permission to live with more joy and intention.

Applying the Word Effect has given me the tools to manage my thoughts, which has led me to learn how to live life on life's terms—the good, the not-so-good, and everything in between. This concept has helped me see that I have the power to keep walking forward despite what happens in my life, making it possible to overcome many obstacles related to health, finances, and personal and professional aspirations. For example, the Word Effect has helped me better handle life-long intermittent bouts of depression and anxiety caused by living either in the past with all its regret and resentment or in the future, filled with worry and uncertainty. It has shown me better ways of dealing with financial uncertainties, such as those our family suffered in 2008 when the real estate market came crashing down. The Word Effect has been the catalyst for finding solutions to some food and body obsessions that progressively got worse the older I got, helping me quit hiding them so I could stop damaging myself and others. It has also helped me overcome many personal insecurities, including those related to the writing of this book, and has been instrumental in finally bringing this publication to fruition!

The Word Effect has also given me the courage to explore new thoughts and ideas, one of which included launching a new retail clothing venture. With no education or experience in business and no outside financial investment, I partnered with my amazing sister-in-law to create Becoming Threads, a successful positive-message apparel company. This project proved to be an important step that put me on a path toward making my secret desire of becoming a public speaker, author, and life coach a reality. Today I am able to share the significance of the power of words with people who want to make positive change and are ready to create the life they have always wanted to live.

And ultimately, the Word Effect is what helped me accept and embrace, with joy, my life as the mother of five boys (we had one more son after boy number four!). While I had never expected my story to include the fact that I would be an "all-boys" mom, the Word Effect helped me decide how I would think about this circumstance so I could stop resisting my life and start living it with gratitude and acceptance.

When Trevor Ryan was born on May 18, 2005, five months after that pivotal day on the ultrasound table, I fell absolutely in love with him—his full head of brown hair, olive skin, and perfect button nose. I have adored him every day since. I can't even imagine what life would be like without him (or any of my sons). My circumstance didn't change, but thanks to the Word Effect, I decided to "put on" new thoughts about my circumstance. (I'll explain more about what "putting on" thoughts and words means later in this introduction.) This new thought process ultimately changed how I perceived my life: it became amazing because Trevor and my other four boys were in it. I was always supposed to be a boy mom; I just didn't know it until it happened. I absolutely love it today and would not change it for anything—not even a girl.

Has everything been perfect for me since applying the Word Effect? Of course not. Life is still a journey of progress and not perfection. But I have shared these successes to show how my life story has been awakened to the possibility of healing, hope, happiness, and health through the power of words—how I began living the life I always wanted to live not with willpower, but with word power! Through this awakening, I know deep in my soul that words matter and that you can transform your life as well. Perhaps through the power of words, your life will transform from one of defeat, distraction, and discontent to one of beauty and purpose.

I want you to know that I believe this potential is real for you even if you are at the lowest place you've ever been in your life. It's possible even if you have picked yourself up multiple times only to fall back down in defeat over a particularly troubling habit. It's conceivable even if you've lost your job, lost your only love, or lost a beautiful child. It's true when none of your expectations for your life seem to be panning out. It's true even when facing a frightening medical diagnosis, or when you can't stop eating, sleeping, or shopping . . . and yes, even during all the shame and guilt you feel overall this shame and guilt!

The powerful effect words can have on you doesn't take away all your problems, but it certainly can help you step into living your story with more grace and hope. It's what allows you to keep moving forward rather than getting stuck when life gets hard.

> *No matter where you are right now, you already have within you what it takes to create your most beautiful life with the power of words.*

The idea that words matter and have the power to affect change is not a new idea. But once I experienced that power in my own life, it created a shift in the way I perceived how my story was unfolding, and I knew I needed to share this idea with people like you! It is my hope that my experiences and the influential stories of others you will read throughout this book will help you come to know, deep within yourself, how the Word Effect can bring you hope, joy, and transformation. I want to show you how the simple act of intentionally choosing words to "put on" each day can truly change your thinking, which will change how you feel, which will ultimately give you the power to change your story for the better.

"Put On" Empowering Words and Thoughts

As a mom of five boys who all grew up playing baseball, I spent much of my free time and evenings enjoying their games. During one game, the idea for launching Becoming Threads, my inspirational apparel company, came to me. I was becoming more and more aware of the power of words, so I really wanted to find a few casual, positive message T-shirts to wear to the games. I figured that wearing positive words would remind me to think positive words, too. Of course, messaging on T-shirts was nothing new—there was no shortage of printed tees in the world. But what I wanted were cute tops for women imprinted with positive messages. I envisioned these powerful words on especially soft fabric, with colors and designs that would be fun and stylish while being comfortable to wear at such places as my kids' baseball games.

On a trip for our seventeenth wedding anniversary, I told my husband that all I wanted was to find some of these tees. But you know how it is when you want something . . . you tend to not be able to find it! That's exactly what happened to me. I went to dozens of stores during our trip but found no tops that met my criteria. I didn't want a brand logo tee or one with sarcastic or irreverent expressions, but that was all I could find.

In the coming weeks, the idea continued to press upon my mind. One day I was shopping with a friend, still looking for these tops, and came upon a T-shirt that had these words printed on it: ALRIGHT, ALRIGHT, ALRIGHT. As I pulled the shirt off the rack to inspect it, I felt as if the heavens opened and had this thought: "Why don't you start putting positive messaging on T-shirts yourself?" I instantly knew this was one of my purposes in life and began developing my idea into a company. My shirts, each printed with a simple, positive message, empower the women who wear them to create their beautiful life.

Creating this company has changed the way I associate with words. I see these printed tees as more than just a reminder to think positively. When I put on a T-shirt with positive messages, I imagine that I am figuratively putting the words on my brain and heart as well. The words aren't just what people see on the outside; they reflect who I am becoming on the inside. These words matter! Just like I send a message to others about who I am when I put on a shirt, my brain sends a message to me about who I am when it "puts on" words. When those words are negative, I believe negative things about myself and hinder my ability to feel happy or be at my best. But when I "put on" positive words, I believe positive things about myself, and suddenly I feel happier and can perform far better.

We'll learn more about how our thoughts affect our actions and results later in the book, but for now, I want you to consider how it feels to "put on" words on the inside. Just as you consider what clothes to wear each day according to your activities and the weather, ask yourself, "What words do I choose to put on today?" Make this as much a part of your routine as you do brushing your teeth or putting on your shoes before you leave the house. Throughout the rest of this book, we'll be learning about seven Power Words that you can put on just like a T-shirt. Those words will influence how you think, feel, and act, empowering you and allowing you to create your beautiful life.

Ditch Willpower for Word Power

As I stated earlier, words do have power, but they don't really mean anything until you make them mean something. As a life and confidence coach, I have come to learn (and now teach to others) that the words you think, read, listen to, and talk about affect your thoughts, which then create your feelings. Your feelings determine the actions you take, which ultimately decide the kind of life you are going to lead.

Whatever you are facing right now—whether it's depression and anxiety, health concerns, parenting woes, financial struggles, a pressing decision you need to make, a behavior you wish to change, or loneliness and isolation—those circumstances have most assuredly been affected by the words you think about every day. If you're not happy with where your life is headed, stay with me as I demonstrate how the Word Effect can help you change those unwanted thoughts (words) that are not serving you so you can create your most beautiful life.

The Word Effect works by giving you a process for living that can help you . . .

- Become more aware of the words you "put on" yourself each day and whether they are forming a negative bias in you of which you aren't aware.
- Apply seven Power Words (explored in the coming chapters), which form the basis of the Word Effect concept. These words are the key to consciously and intentionally focusing your thoughts and feelings where they need to be to affect powerful change and positive movement forward.
- Understand how consistency matters and how to establish patterns of persistent behavior that will allow you to fully embrace your life and all that it holds for you, one little word at a time.

Let me demonstrate further, through my personal experience, how the Word Effect works.

Before I discovered the Word Effect, I spent most of my life trying to move forward linearly by relying on sheer willpower. Constantly exerting willpower always had me thinking that if I could only get to a certain point in my life when I could arrive at a certain place (when I got to have my baby girl, for instance, or when I had lost enough weight, or when my boys had mastered certain life skills), then I would begin to feel a particular way and could finally live a life of joy and contentment.

But this willpower approach was like struggling to reach a mirage of water in a lonely desert. I would push and push to get to that glistening goal, only to discover that the "water" was not really there for me to drink; it had appeared at a distance again thanks to the words I was constantly thinking and the feelings those thoughts generated. I felt stuck, never making any real progress.

But the Word Effect showed me that my approach to life was not working on a linear path. Instead, I discovered that life's journey progresses in a circular motion. This idea is illustrated in following this circle.

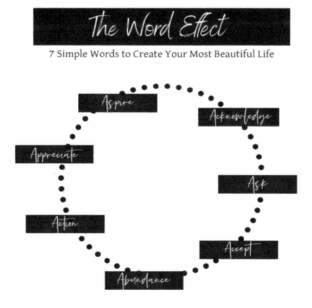

Why use a circle to illustrate the Word Effect? Because the act of creating a beautiful life is not linear but rather a circular, never-ending process. In this pattern, we constantly move forward, make progress, and then start the cycle over again with each new circumstance, relationship, problem, or decision. And if you want to become your best self, you must constantly progress *upward* in that circular movement. As you experience being human, you are always starting over, establishing new beginnings, and creating new opportunities for inquiry, discovery, growth, change, and progression. There is no finish line. You are forever renewing this cycle with each new lesson, and each new circumstance.

The seven simple Power Words of the Word Effect cycle keep me moving forward as I move through the cycle over and over. When I feel stuck, these words help me discover where I am on the circular path and how to work through that position until I am ready to step forward again. As you apply the seven Power Words just as I have—in this circular, forward motion—you will begin to see more clearly how to manage the thoughts and feelings you attach to the facts of your life.

As we begin this journey together, I encourage you right now to look very closely at your heart. What words are you focused on? Are you stuck, regressing backward, or are you moving forward? Stephen R. Covey, the author of *The 7 Habits of Highly Effective People,* has said this about the influence of words: "Words are, and always have been, the creative force of the universe. . . . Used correctly and positively, words are the first building blocks for success and inner peace; they provide the vision and focus that show the way to growth and contribution. Used incorrectly and negatively, they are capable of undermining even the best of intentions. This is true in business, in personal relationships, and in every other walk of life." Yes, words literally have the power to create or destroy! If you feel like your life isn't building in the direction you want, it's probably because of the words you're choosing to focus on.

Let's take another look at what it means for words to have creative power. I love what John 1:1 of the Bible says: "In the beginning was the Word, and the Word was with God. And the Word was God." God's Word is the most powerful creative force of all. Once that idea clicked in my head, I realized that my willpower wasn't going to be enough to help me create the life I always desired and overcome the destructive patterns I'd found myself in. Finally, I went to the source of all power and asked God for help. When I did, He sent a friend who asked me one simple question: "Becky, why don't you stop wondering 'why' and start asking 'how' to deal with your life situation instead?" When I followed her advice, God was able to help me experience for myself that change was possible—not through willpower, but through word power.

As I have asked *how* to change my words instead of constantly asking *why* my circumstances are the way they are, my life has become so much more beautiful. If God created the worlds with words, including this beautiful earth upon which we live, He can certainly help you and me create our most beautiful life with words too.

Jim Rohn, a business philosopher, has said, "There are no new fundamentals. Truth is not new—it is old." As I noted earlier, the power of words is not a new idea, but perhaps the idea is new to you—that you already have the power within you to change through the words you choose to think about. Now is the time to see how transformative those words can be and discover how to consistently use them for your good.

I want to give you permission now, just as my friend did for me when she suggested I stop asking "why," to ditch willpower and turn instead to word power. It's time to stop wishing and start living! My secret desire to share my story with you and become a writer, speaker, and coach is happening through my very own story of discovery. Today, I am a living example of my own work. I know that words matter, and I feel blessed to be able to share that truth with you.

You and I can decide what words we put on each day. I invite you to begin now to immerse yourself in the seven Power Words we will be exploring in the upcoming chapters. Begin to experience the influence of the Word Effect, just as I have, so you can create your most beautiful life.

Now, let's get started!

CHAPTER 1

BECOMING AWARE OF YOUR WORDS

"You can spend the time distressed, discontent, distracted, discouraged, dissatisfied or you can spend the time enjoying, engaging, enriched.
The only decision you have to make today is what you do with your time."
—Ann Voskamp

A year before my fortieth birthday, I found myself crying to my husband one evening after the kids were in bed about how I had lost my willpower. What had happened to me? Why couldn't I set a goal and stick to it? Why was I so sad and unhappy? One thing I was sure about: my life was definitely not unfolding how I had planned. Questions swirled around in my mind about where my life was headed. What was I doing wrong? Did God not love me enough to help me achieve my heart's desires?

As I discussed all these things with Kris, I began to see that for most of my life, I had been waiting for my circumstances to change so I could be happy. "If only my kids would keep their rooms clean the way I want them cleaned, then I could enjoy the beautiful house I live in," I would think. Or "If only my husband made more money, then I could enjoy my lifestyle a little more." The more I got, the more it seemed I needed. I was unable to be content with what I had, always chasing the next thing that might make me happy. I was living a life of "if only" instead of being full of gratitude and thankfulness for what was. I was living a life of procrastination, perfectionism, and self-pity—the result of the words I chose to associate with the circumstances of my life. I subconsciously put on negative words each day that caused overwhelming feelings to dominate my life. When I felt overwhelmed, a downward cycle of confusion set in, and I became distracted by anxiety, self-pity, victimhood, frustration, dissatisfaction, and discontent, among other things. This cycle of negative thinking affected every area of my life.

At this time, I was the mother of five amazing boys, aged sixteen to four. I had been married to my high school sweetheart for seventeen years and was serving in my church and community. I lived in a comfortable home and had all of my needs met and even enjoyed many of my wants. Life was supposed to be good . . . so why was I so dissatisfied, so discontented?

The distracted, negative anxiety that ruled my life far more than I wanted, had more than likely started in childhood. I had always been a fearful girl, invariably waiting for the axe to fall or the other shoe to drop, or the next bad thing to happen. If I was given two situations to look at, I always "knew" the bad one of the two would occur. Then if calamity struck, I would beat myself up and ask what I had done wrong or why God had allowed the crisis to happen.

As I unloaded my fears on my husband, I realized my life had been full of a lot of negative self-talk. I had tons of "chatter" in my head, and it was almost always fear-driven. All these words were relentlessly telling me I wasn't worthy of something good, and if I worked only a little harder, I could stop being anxious and dissatisfied and finally achieve what I wanted. Like a thirsty wanderer in a desert, I was always looking ahead to a mirage, forgetting I had already packed a bottle of water in my backpack. I was constantly searching for more instead of noticing what I had with me all along.

This incessant lack of contentment was completely the opposite of how my husband looked at the world. Early in our marriage, I noticed a distinct difference between Kris and myself—our perception was very different on almost everything. While he viewed the glass as half full, I was more "realistic," or as it is probably more accurately called, pessimistic. The difference between us is perfectly defined in a quote by the thirty-third US president, Harry S. Truman: "A pessimist is one who makes difficulties of his opportunities, and an optimist is one who makes opportunities of his difficulties."

I was always complaining about how hard things were, and because misery loves company, I took it upon myself to be sure to bring my husband's feet back down to earth where they belonged. My negativity had an effect on everyone I came in contact with, especially those I lived with. I knew how to put on a happy face around others and tried to keep the negativity from seeping out of my mouth the best I could, but within the walls of my home, it flowed freely. If the words swirling around in my head were negative and caused me to feel like reaching for the stars was useless, well, I had best keep everyone near me down as well, right?

The truth is I had become completely distracted by all the negativity and anxiety I had unconsciously and unknowingly allowed to rule my life. Not only was I a "natural" pessimist, it seemed, but I was becoming a cynic as well, suspicious of everyone and everything, the judgmental kind of person I never thought I would be. Each day I used fearful words to define my feelings, which ultimately clouded my mind and took my attention away from all my blessings and the goodness of others. Subconsciously, in an attempt to manage the constant anxiety I felt, I had decided that if I could control others, then I could better handle my own lack of control over myself, thereby avoiding having to work on *myself*.

As I opened up and spilled all my feelings out on Kris, I heard him speak words I have never forgotten. In a kind and gentle way, he said, "It seems like whatever you have in your life, you are always wanting more. You never seem satisfied with where you are today." My first reaction to this was, "No, you just don't understand—if you had to live how I do, you would feel this way too." But little by little, I began to see that his words were truer than I realized. As I allowed myself to really ponder on his perspective, my heart felt a glimpse of hope again, something I had not felt in a long time. That hope stemmed from the thought that just knowing the cause of all these unhappy feelings might ultimately result in me finding a solution to them. Was the power to change within me all along?

As I became aware of words such as *distraction*, *despair*, and *discontent* whirling about in my head, I began to see just how powerful words can be, and how much the words I put on myself every day were beating me up. I resolved that all the anxiety in my life—caused by my distracted state of discontent—would have to be reduced drastically. At the point of making this realization, I asked myself this question: Do I have the power within to change my story? I wanted to look for someone else to do all that changing for me, but I instead felt the nudge to look inward.

With Kris's words ringing in my ears, I cried out to God in my helplessness (and a sense of hopefulness) for answers. As I did, a thought came to me: "Change your words." I now know that thought came from my Heavenly Father, but at the time, I didn't fully realize it. It was just a thought, but I felt it impress upon my mind and heart, unlike any I had felt for a very long time. I initially had a strange sense of curiosity that compelled me to explore this concept further, and my exploring ultimately enabled me to discover the Word Effect. The cycle of the seven Power Words, which we will be exploring in the coming chapters, worked in my life to change everything about it.

If you're reading this book, it's likely that you, too, have experienced the kind of negative, discontented feelings I was having in my life. No doubt, just as was the case for me, such feelings have resulted from the words you have chosen to think regarding your given circumstances.

To help you gain a more hopeful and positive perspective on your own life and take full advantage of the power the Word Effect can have on you, let's take a closer look at where the negative words you are likely thinking come from.

Negativity Begets Negativity

At first glance, it may seem that most of the unpleasant things in your life have just randomly occurred. But I want to encourage you to consider a different possibility:

Most of what you fear, hate, or want to avoid in your life is likely because of the negative way in which you feel about what is happening to you or around you, and those feelings are the result of the words you choose to think about those happenings.

That's a pretty bold statement, but it's one I'm confident I can back up. As a life coach, I use the following model with my clients to show how feelings and words affect actions, which then determine outcomes. The outcomes you are experiencing in your life, whether good or bad, are the result of your thoughts (which comprise very specific words you are focusing on). If you take a closer look at the words you choose to use in defining what's happening to you, you will find they will correlate almost perfectly with the outcomes you are experiencing, either good or bad.

Here Is What It Looks Like...

CIRCUMSTANCES
CAN TRIGGER

THOUGHTS
CAUSE

FEELINGS
DRIVE

ACTIONS
CREATE

RESULTS

I'm sure you've heard the old adage, "Negativity begets negativity." Research indicates the truth of these simple words. Paul Rozin and Edward B. Royzman, psychology professors at the University of Pennsylvania, have created a theory about what they call "negativity bias." In their research, they hypothesize that humans are predisposed to give more attention to negative thinking: "There is a general bias, based on both innate predispositions and experience, in animals and humans, to give greater weight to negative entities (e.g., events, objects, personal traits)."

Several other experts seem to agree. According to Kendra Cherry, author of *The Everything Psychology Book*, evidence indicates that we humans tend to obsess about the awful instead of the beautiful. Have you ever found yourself dwelling on an insult or fixating on your mistakes?

"Criticisms often have a greater impact than compliments and bad news frequently draws more attention than good."

Criticisms often have a greater impact than compliments, and bad news frequently draws more attention than good," says Cherry. "The reason for this is that negative events have a greater impact on our brains than positive ones. Psychologists refer to this as negative bias or negativity bias, and it can have a powerful effect on your behavior, your decisions, and even your relationships." Cherry shares five things we tend to do as humans experiencing negative bias:

1. Remember traumatic experiences better than positive ones.
2. Recall insults more than praise.
3. React more strongly to negative stimuli.
4. Think about negative things more frequently than positive things.
5. Respond more strongly to negative events than to equally positive ones.

Margaret Jaworski, in her article for *Remedy Health Media* entitled "The Negativity Bias: Why the Bad Stuff Sticks," notes, "Not only do negative events and experiences import more quickly, but they also linger longer than positive ones. The negativity bias can even cause you to dwell on something negative even if something positive is equally or more present."

This negativity bias, also known as the "negativity effect" according to Wikipedia, is the idea that negative happenings, including "unpleasant thoughts, emotions, or social interactions, [and] harmful/

traumatic events have a greater effect on one's psychological state and processes than neutral or positive things. In other words, something very positive will generally have less of an impact on a person's behavior and cognition than something equally emotional but negative."

Research clearly shows that negativity will grow if we allow it. "In most interactions, we are more likely to notice negative things and later remember them more vividly," Cherry continues. "This bias toward the negative leads you to pay much more attention to the bad things that happen, making them seem much more important than they really are."

As I learned about this "negativity bias," which some people (like me, it seems) appear to be more wired for than others, I saw a pattern. My habits of negativity bias were like a thin thread slowly wrapping itself around my throat: over time, it gained enough strength to keep me bound in negativity virtually all the time. My attention was constantly being drawn to habitual skepticism.

Negativity had become a habit to me, so with each new decision and situation, I didn't stop to think about the words I was using to process what was happening. I didn't realize I could carefully choose an appropriate focus with new words; I just allowed the negativity to cycle in my thoughts over and over again. Only when I became more aware of the negativity bias born out of the words I chose to think and became more deliberate with my thoughts each day did I start to see things change.

The apple doesn't fall far from the tree, and the negativity bias I was suffering from was beginning to manifest in my kids as well. My oldest son, a senior in high school, was handsome, smart, and a member of the school's baseball team. Everything appeared to be going well for him. But he began to struggle too.

I had been praying to know how I could help my son, and while dusting a bookcase in my living room one day, I had the thought, "Invite Kayden to join the church choir and sing the Christmas songs in preparation for the Christmas program." *What?* Invite my eighteen-year-old son to do *what?*

I totally questioned this inspiration but decided to sit with it and not make a quick decision either way. A few days later, driving in the car with just Kayden, the thought came again: "Invite him now!" I knew I wanted to obey that prompting, so I mustered up the courage to suggest that the power of words and music might help him feel better. He looked at me and, without much resistance, said, "Sure, I'll try it."

Almost a year later, in October of 2017, he was speaking in church as he prepared to leave to serve a two-year service mission in Sacramento, California. As he spoke, he shared his experiences of singing in the church choir. I didn't realize how much impact the power of words had ultimately had on him until that moment.

"A little before last Christmas, I was kind of down on myself. I wasn't happy," Kayden began. "I felt like I didn't have any friends. I just wasn't myself. And for some reason, my mom told me she had been prompted to invite me to sing in the choir. Surprisingly I said, sure! I don't really love to sing, or know how to sing, or have an amazing talent, but I did it. And honestly, I loved it.

I loved singing in the Christmas program. I loved practicing and performing, and for some reason, it made me happy. Each week I would look forward to practice. So, I kept singing once the Christmas program was over and have sung for the last year, 'cause why not keep doing something that makes you feel better? I'm not suggesting we all need to join the choir to be happy, but I am suggesting maybe we can all try to do something that is out of our comfort zone that will uplift us or others."

Kayden found a way to combat the negativity bias he was experiencing by putting the power of words expressed through song to work. When he put uplifting and powerful words about truth and Jesus Christ in his life as he read and sang the music, he was able to totally change the way his negative thought processes were dragging him down, and he became a much happier person. Kayden and I have since talked more about this experience, and both of us realized that this was the moment when the Word Effect began to take hold in his life—when it became a way for him to regain power over the negativity bias that was setting him back.

"Emotional Childishness" Keeps Us Stuck in Negativity

The ability to see our own negativity bias can be difficult. Our parents may or may not have taught us to be aware of the words we think about when processing our feelings. Few classes are offered in high school or college that teach how to become an emotionally intelligent grown-up. Once we have reached adulthood, our brains should be developed enough to understand how our thoughts and feelings are formed. As adults, we are capable of reflecting on our thoughts, and therefore we can decide what to think and what to feel at any given moment, no matter what is going on around us. But this thought pattern doesn't always occur automatically for everyone. When we cannot objectively analyze our own thought processes, we remain in what master life coach Brooke Castillo calls "emotional childhood."

"Emotional childhood occurs when grown adults have not matured past childhood in terms of managing their emotions," says Castillo. "This means they react to their emotions, act out, or avoid emotions rather than taking full responsibility and choosing thoughts that will create more desirable and appropriate emotions. In short, emotional childhood is not taking responsibility for how you feel."

If you are stuck in emotional childhood, it is likely that you are un-aware of the words you choose to think about or put on each day, which then affects how you feel, which ultimately drives the choices you make. This lack of cognizance about your emotions may be the reason you feel stuck and can't move forward. I know that was the case for me—the words and thoughts I was focusing on daily kept me chained to my negativity bias.

For example, my anxiety and negativity grew as each new child came into our family because I chose to live more emotionally childish than emotionally mature. Motherhood never seemed easy for me, at least not in those early years, and I didn't naturally slip into this role. It was something I did because I wanted to but also because I felt obligated to do so. As a perfectionist in denial, I had a plan for my life detailing how I wanted things to unfold with my parenting. I was sure that when I saw other young children show up to church with a runny nose, for instance, or be sent off to school with their hair uncombed, I would never be that type of mom. I had a plan to be different. But when things didn't go according to plan, my emotional child took over, along with negative words and feelings about what was happen-ing "to me" that didn't fit my expectations.

When my oldest began preparing to get his driver's license, I thought, "Okay, the state of Utah might think he can drive . . . but I sure don't." I had no plans to let him drive. I heard other moms talk about how great it was to have another driver in the house who could get them-selves home from their own practice or stop to get a gallon of milk at the store. Yet I remember thinking, "I had better just pick the milk up myself, because what if my son hit the car next to him as he pulled into the parking lot? What if he caused an accident?"

So instead of giving him the opportunity to grow, I decided I would keep doing those things for him—the things that allowed me to feel in control and not have to deal with all the negative, fearful emotions I had to face with this new "driving teenager" situation. Unfortunate-ly, living in this emotionally childish state of needing to feel safe and not having to process my thoughts and emotions created a problem: I stopped living.

Since I wasn't aware of my own negativity bias, my brain had to de-vise a way to take control of situations that were not going the way I wanted them to. Rather than reflect on my thoughts and how they might be affecting my parenting decisions, I resorted to control tactics instead. The older my kids grew, the more I wanted to control each and every situation in their lives. I was again trying to manipulate the circumstances around me.

I thought it was easier to change everyone else than to just focus on myself. For me, it was much easier raising little ones in diapers than teenagers because when they were little, I had complete control over them. They did what I needed them to do when I wanted them to do it because they had no other choice. But with their maturity came newfound independence, which only stirred up more fear in my heart as I realized I would no longer be able to make every decision for them. This frightened me because I was not aware of how my nega-tive thoughts drove me to control family situations as a way to avoid dealing with my feelings.

I teach my coaching clients that the brain is wired to offer three thoughts to us first: to seek pleasure, avoid pain, and conserve energy (or do what is easiest). The brain does this in order to protect us. The article "The Negativity Bias in User Experience" by the Nielsen Norman Group illustrates with this simple story how fixating on negativity is a way the brain tries to protect itself from perceived danger:

> *Imagine you went on a beautiful hike and along the trail you encountered a rattlesnake. What do you think you will remember more vividly about the hike: the snake you encountered or the beautiful scenery along the way? Most people will remember the rattlesnake incident better, because negative experiences tend to affect them much more than positive ones. This is an example of negativity bias. Bad news or negative traits signal danger. From an evolutionary perspective, learning to identify potentially hazardous situations was vital for survival in a harsh environment rich in predators. While today's world has arguably fewer threats, humans are still wired for self-preservation.*

In dwelling on the negative aspects of my son learning to drive, I was unconsciously trying to avoid pain; my brain was tricking me into thinking that by doing so I was keeping everyone safe. But if we don't question these thoughts at times, we will stop living the life we are meant to live and will unintentionally decide to make everyone close to us stop living as well.

When I told my husband about my fear of having our son begin driving, he just looked at me curiously and said, "Becky, you know that is why we have car insurance, right? You have to let him try. The only way he will learn is if he tries." This concept of letting my child spread his wings baffled my mind because I had determined it was better to just stay where we were than to move forward into unknown and scary territory.

Through all this fear and anxiety surrounding my teenage son's natural development, I thought about when I turned sixteen and how my parents had likely had many of these same fears and concerns about me. I bet my mom and dad didn't think I was ready to move forward and head out to drive either, but they let go of those fears and let me grow anyway. Of course, ultimately, I wanted my son to drive and experience life as well, so I had to consciously make the choice to stop functioning as an emotional child by becoming more aware of the negative bias affecting my thoughts and feelings surrounding the situation.

The only way to become an emotional adult is through taking self-responsibility for first, your thoughts, and second, your feelings. "We are responsible for how we feel in every moment," Brooke Castillo says. "We are in charge of how we think, we are in charge of how we feel. When we are functioning as emotional children, we are blaming other people [or circumstances] for how we feel, how we act, and for the results, we get in our life."

According to a popular reference, often cited in articles on human thought management and attributed to 2005 National Science Foundation (NSF) research, the average person has about twelve thousand to sixty thousand thoughts per day. Of those thousands of thoughts, it is said, 80 percent are negative, and 95 percent are exactly the same, repetitive thoughts as the day before. "We can see that one of the tendencies of the mind is to focus on the negative and 'play the same songs' over and over again," a 2021 TLEX Institute article noted about the NSF claim.

And the TLEX article also cites popular research commonly attributed to a 2005 Cornell University study, which found that 85 percent of what we worry about never happens. "Of the 15 percent of the worries that did happen, 79 percent of the subjects discovered that either they could handle the difficulty better than expected, or that the difficultly taught them a lesson worth learning," the article goes on to claim. "The conclusion is that 97 percent of our worries are baseless and result from an unfounded pessimistic perception."

Such findings point to the fact that words matter! With the human brain asserted to have up to sixty thousand thoughts a day, imagine how many of those thoughts are caused by a *set of negative words* you may be repeating over and over in your head. This idea bears repeating:

> *Imagine how many of your thoughts are caused by a* **set of negative** *words you may be repeating over and over in your head!*

Perhaps that set of words is preventing you from taking responsibility for your feelings, forcing you to live in emotional childhood. How much is a habitual cycle of negative thinking affecting your ability to create the kind of life you were meant to lead?

Breaking Free of a Negative Bias

If you've become comfortable with your own negativity bias (which I will wager has likely been formed by a repeated *set of words*), it can be hard to change the way you react to life—I can personally vouch for that! I once read how pigs are content to just lie around in the mud. Why would any animal choose to just lie in the mud all day? Surely, they want more out of life than that?

But to get out of the mud, a pig must first muster the energy to stand up, to have the idea that there is a better place to be. Once a pig stands up and the discomfort sets in, some unknown feelings begin to surface—feelings of cold from the air hitting his wet, mud-stained body, feelings of the effort and energy it takes to move to another spot— and before you know it, the pig decides to just lie back down. It thinks, "You know, I like lying in the mud. It is safe, it is comfortable, and it requires little effort; I think I am happy right here." The pig begins to look around at every other pig, and they appear to be happy just lying in the mud as well. "Maybe this is all I need," the pig concludes.

As you allow yourself to be more and more distracted by your own negativity bias that is likely keeping you stuck in emotional child-hood, you can become much like the pig, stuck in the mud, wishing, and hoping for more out of life but perhaps unwilling to do anything different to get there. That was how I felt before I discovered the Word Effect and began taking a different approach to life. Each time I would stand up to make a change, I felt uncomfortable, unpleasant, and unsure. Before I took even a step or two forward, I quickly quit on myself. Negative thoughts and the set of negative words chattering in my head drove me deeper into the mud.

Perhaps you have felt this way as well. Maybe you have wanted to get out of the mud, but the discomfort of doing so was too much, or you didn't know how. I'm here to tell you, you don't have to be stuck in emotional childhood with all your negative biases affecting your ability to live a beautiful life. You can determine to put on new words, and new thoughts that can help you feel hope.

The best way to choose a new, positive, and hopeful word set is through living the Word Effect. Through the process of applying a new set of positive words—the Word Effect's seven Power Words—you can learn, as I did, how to look at life as an emotionally intelligent adult and become more aware of your own negativity bias. You have the power to become the CEO of your own thoughts and emotions.

You have a choice! The power to change is within you. Words matter! You can create the life you have always desired with the power of *your* words. In the coming chapters, centered on each of the seven Power Words, you will learn how to live in emotional adulthood so you can do the following:

- Take responsibility for your pain and for your joy.
- Stop expecting other people to "make" you happy.
- Stop expecting others to "make" you feel secure.
- Appreciate that you are the only person who can hurt your feelings, stop yourself from moving forward, or look at life through a lens of fear and anxiety. You do so with the words you choose to think and the feelings those words and thoughts generate.

Through the Word Effect, you can become aware of the way you think about and look at any situation in life. It will give you the power you need to decide with full clarity where you are in your thought processes and what you need to do to move forward.

In the next chapter, we will begin exploring the Power Words that I now live by and invite you to live by as well. These words will bring you new purpose, goodness, healing, and more love. There is real power in this set of words. They have given me the ability to step out of the mud and live the life I have always desired. These words have helped me loosen the grip of negativity that was choking me.

To help prepare you to begin freeing yourself from the hold that a negativity bias might be having over you, I want to encourage you to take the following simple challenge. Use this as an opportunity to look at yourself and see how much you are affected by the words you are thinking and how they might be preventing you from living your best and most beautiful life. Don't settle for one more day living distracted and discontent—get on the road toward becoming your best *you* today!

Challenge Your Own Negativity Bias

Do words matter? You bet! Remember the popular claim attributed to the NSF that we can have up to sixty thousand thoughts per day, and close to 80 percent of those will be negative? To find out how much of your life is affected by a negativity bias, you must become more cognizant of how many of the words you think are negative or fearful.

1. Pick one day this week when you can devote much of your time to being aware of your thoughts and writing down the words that comprise those thoughts. All day long, write down every word that comes to your mind about situations, feelings, conversations, problems, and opportunities that crop up. Then, at the end of the day, do the following:

   a. Tally how many of the words you used to describe your thoughts were negative and how many were positive.

   b. Out of the negative words, identify those that came up the most. This will identify a negative "word set" your mind seems to use over and over.

Now you should be aware of the word set you are most commonly using that is instilling the negativity bias you continue to focus on.

"Decisions are the ultimate power we have in our lives!
A simple decision is simply a commitment to a thought,
feeling and action that creates a result."
—Brooke Castillo

Are you ready to ditch your thinking problem with a simple solution? Discover "The One Word Way"? It is my free eBook that offers three of the most toxic words you might be using daily, and not realizing how they often hold you back from creating the life you always desired. By changing these three words, you will have the opportunity to breathe life back into your story, which will allow you to grow and expand with possibility.

Plus, you will get simple follow-up teachings and emails that are positive and proactive perspective shifts toward living life on life's terms.

If you're ready to discover how your words matter—Join me here.

www.becomingwithbecky.com/join

CHAPTER 2

ACKNOWLEDGE

THE FIRST STEP TO BECOMING YOUR AUTHENTIC (AND MOST BEAUTIFUL) SELF

"The first step on the path to positive change is acknowledging that change is necessary and possible. Open yourself to the possibility of seeing the world in a new way. What do you have to lose?"
—Alex Blackwell

Power Word 1: *Acknowledge – (verb) to accept or admit the existence or truth of something.*

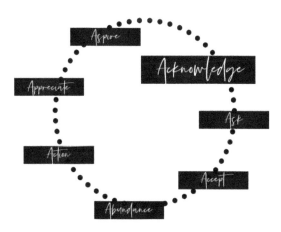

When I was a little girl, I loved eating olives. On the occasions when we had a bowl of olives at dinner, they didn't last long between the eight people in my family. I would get a few, and by the time the bowl got back to me, the olives would be gone.

One afternoon when I was about nine, my mom and dad were out, and I was home alone. I saw an unopened can of olives in the pantry and had a great idea—I could take the can opener outside with the olives and eat the entire can by myself. I would not need to share or ration with anyone. The olives would be all mine! So I snuck outside, opened the can, and began eating. I ate and ate and ate, and then something happened: I got incredibly sick. I didn't realize that I could just stop eating and put the remaining olives in the fridge for later. No, I had made a plan to eat them and somehow felt I needed to stick with this plan, even if it meant giving myself a stomachache. After gobbling the olives all up, I discarded the evidence for fear of getting in trouble for doing such a foolish thing.

Why was I so afraid to just tell my mom I wanted to eat some olives? Looking back, I believe she would have said yes to my request, but at that moment, I was hesitant to acknowledge something I desired because I feared the answer wouldn't be what I wanted. Why was it so hard to admit that I liked olives and often desired to have a few? We had several cans in the pantry; it wasn't like this was the last can of olives I would ever see in my lifetime. But the way I saw it as a child, I needed to sneak—to take what I wanted and hide my actions instead of just admitting my desires. As a little girl, I just didn't like getting in trouble, and I especially didn't enjoy being told no. So I decided early on that if I thought the answer might be "not at all," then I would go around that opposition and make sure I got "all of it."

Avoiding conflict and not wanting to displease others only became more of a problem for me as I grew older. Once when I was about eleven or twelve, I did something that upset my dad. He scolded me and called me "Rebecca Jane," my full name, which was only used by my parents when I was in trouble. I can't even remember what I'd done, but what I do remember about this incident is the shame and guilt I felt for disappointing him, for letting my mom down, and for letting myself down, as well as the agony I felt about it all.

I remember very clearly making a conscious decision at that time to always do what my parents asked so I could avoid getting in trouble in the future. This is where the seeds of perfectionism were sown in me—early on; I had the makings of a people-pleaser while being very dishonest with myself about who I really was and what I truly desired. I wanted to be anyone and everyone besides me. I fell into the trap of comparing myself to others and always desired what they had because, somehow, the real Becky wasn't enough.

My perfectionistic tendencies seemed to develop insidiously without my realizing the crippling effects they would ultimately have on me. The word *perfectionist* is sneaky because although it sounds useful, it is exactly the opposite. This need to be perfect is what author and researcher Brené Brown describes as a self-destructive and addictive belief system: "Perfectionism . . . fuels this primary thought: If I look perfect, and do everything perfectly, I can avoid or minimize the painful feelings of shame, judgment, and blame."

But as humans, we are put on earth to make mistakes and then learn from them. We are all flawed in the eyes of our Creator, and we must learn from our experiences so we can become our most authentic (and, consequently, beautiful) version. Brené notes that this need to avoid all mistakes comes from a fear of vulnerability.

"We live in a vulnerable world, and we numb vulnerability. We are the most in debt, obese, addicted, and medicated adult cohort in US history."
Brené Brown 2010 TED Talk.

I was no different—like a sheep, falling in line like so many others, I numbed my own vulnerability by striving for perfection. Brown continues, "The problem is, you cannot selectively numb emotion. You can't say, 'Here's the bad stuff. Here are vulnerability, shame, fear, and disappointment. I don't want to feel these.' When we numb those, we numb joy, gratitude, and happiness [as well], and then we feel miserable."

When we're unable to admit and acknowledge that we need help, then we are bound and determined to make absolute perfection our partner, and sadly, no true and lasting change can ever occur. "Perfectionism, after all, is an ultimately self-defeating way to move through the world," said Brené in her book *The Gifts of Imperfection*. "It is built on an excruciating irony—making and admitting mistakes is a necessary part of growing and learning and being human. . . . By avoiding mistakes at any cost, a perfectionist can make it harder to reach their own lofty goals."

Anne Wilson Schaef, American clinical psychologist, and author of the book *When Society Becomes an Addict*, said, "Perfectionism is self-abuse of the highest order." And the author of *Big Magic*, Elizabeth Gilbert, stated in her book, "Perfection is unachievable: It's a myth and a trap and a hamster wheel that will run you to death."

As I matured, my brain struggled to be honest with myself about what I wanted, what I desired, and who I was. When I was with my parents, I tried to please them; when I was with my friends, I would adjust my behavior to be what I perceived they wanted from me so I could feel more accepted. This fear of not belonging prohibited me from feeling real love for myself and, consequently, others. This need to be something other than myself was destroying my authenticity. I was constantly behind a mask of perfectionism—which Brené calls "other-focused," where we worry, "What will they think?" She explains that "perfectionism is not to be confused with healthy striving, which is self-focused [and asks] 'how can I improve?'"

I continued to live a chameleon life as I moved from my teenage years into adulthood, trying to keep everyone happy around me. The problem was, no one was really happy around me because I was not happy myself. The word choices I was thinking by the time I was in my thirties were all negative and degrading. I would never dream of speaking to anyone the way I spoke to myself, yet I didn't stop to consider that I was hurting myself.

Perhaps you can relate.

Have you felt the same kind of anxiety that maybe who you really are is not enough? That you aren't acceptable? That being vulnerable around others and exposing your truest and best self is too dangerous? Perhaps you have been unable to even consider such things, to look at the words swirling around in your head and acknowledge that you might need help. If you're like me, you might be thinking, "I don't have a problem. If only things would change, or if only the people in my life would change, then things would be fine."

Sound familiar?

If so, these thoughts are likely preventing you from making any kind of progress toward a happy and fulfilling life, keeping you stuck in emotional childhood. Such thoughts certainly caused me a lot of pain along the way because it took me so many years to finally *acknowledge* that I even had a problem. My self-destructive perfectionistic thoughts (the words I used to describe myself), which I had been thinking ever since I was a child, had become a core part of my belief system. As an adult I never considered that they might be the reason I was so unhappy and discontent—the reason I had such a strong negativity bias.

As I noted earlier in the book, the thoughts we have over and over again become our beliefs. Your current belief about yourself is based on your thoughts from the past. Beliefs are just thoughts you have put on repeatedly until you stop questioning them and they become a part of you. Master life coach Brooke Castillo teaches, "Just like a fish is unaware of the water in which it swims, we are often unaware of the thoughts we're thinking. We must develop the skill of becoming a 'Watcher' [over] our thoughts. We have to learn to watch our brain think so we can recognize thoughts and beliefs for what they are."

In order to become the watcher of your own thoughts, you must first acknowledge those thoughts. I hope you took the challenge at the end of the last chapter so you could determine the set of words you are using to think about your life. What kind of words are you thinking about yourself each day that define your belief system? Have you identified that set of words? Are you on autopilot when it comes to the way you interact with yourself and with others based on applying that set over and over? Are you willing to accept that the things you are dissatisfied with in your life may be directly related to the words you use to think about your life and everything in it?

I encourage you not to delay in identifying those words. Deciding now what words you are going to put on each day will give you the power to think of new thoughts that will truly serve you. When I started using this first Power Word, *acknowledge*, to admit to myself and to God that the set of negative words I was putting on each day was crippling my life and that I needed help, it became just a bit easier to admit my weaknesses to others. For me, this step proved to be a significant part of making real change.

> *Acknowledging your weaknesses gives you the courage to step out of fear and into authenticity, which brings incredible power. It helps you remember the capacity you already have within you to change, live the life you want and become who you were always meant to be.*

In this chapter, I want to show you why this statement is true by using some of my own personal experiences and the stories of others. I have seen in my own life and now in the lives of many people, including my coaching clients, that it doesn't matter what problem you are looking to solve or what dream or desire you are trying to fulfill. *Acknowledging* those things to yourself, a Higher Power, and to others is the first step toward becoming your authentic self-full of courage, optimism, energy, and power.

Acknowledging Gives You Courage

As I noted in Chapter 1, the outcomes you are experiencing in your life, whether good or bad, are the result of your thoughts (which comprise a very specific set of words you are thinking about). If you take a closer look at the words you choose to think and *acknowledge* what those words are doing to your life, you will feel a surprising amount of positive, courageous energy flow into you. This is because *awareness*, even if it's focused on things you are not very proud of, *is the beginning of change.* And the thought of being able to progress and grow is empowering, and that empowerment brings hope. And when you have hope, you can do what it takes to move forward into a better life.

Marie Forelo has said in her book *Everything Is Figureoutable*, "There can be no significant change in the world unless we first have the courage to change ourselves. In order to change ourselves, we must first believe we can." This is a key component of what it means to acknowledge. When you acknowledge both your strengths and weaknesses, you give yourself permission to believe that you can change those weaknesses into something stronger.

Craig Manning, in his book *The Fearless Mind*, shares how just acknowledging our fear (or problem, issue, desire, etc.) can help us begin to believe different thoughts, which can give us the courage to change how we approach every issue that may be keeping us blocked. Again, our thoughts, or words, create everything! When asked what he was afraid of in a class he was taking for his Ph.D., Manning admitted he was terrified of crocodiles. "I'm from Australia, and crocodiles are aggressive creatures. They will take us even when they are not hungry." This thought had been playing in his head over and over so many times that it had become a belief even though he had never actually been confronted by a crocodile himself.

> My professor . . . [then] asked me to visualize being in a room with no way out except for one door. He [asked me] to visualize a croc coming around the corner [and] what I would likely be thinking about. My response was, "I would be afraid of being bitten and how badly it was going to hurt. The pain, I guess, is what I would be afraid of, and the damage it could do to my body." My mentor went on to explain that all those thoughts were in the future. Fear only exists in our thoughts of what may or may not happen in the future. He then asked, "And what would you be thinking if the croc was actually biting your leg?" I [said] I would be punching, kicking and fighting it.

Manning's conversation with his professor proves that the feeling of fear (which then perpetuates a whole slew of other negative thoughts, feelings, and actions, including perfectionism, self-pity, discontent, the need to control others, shame, and so forth) is caused by our thoughts. And when we feel fear (or any other negative emotion), we show up differently than when we approach a problem with determination (like fighting a crocodile to save our life). We show up with courage rather than cowardice. Acknowledging his fear of crocodiles was the first step Manning had to take in order to overcome that fear. Doing so got him out of a destructive belief system (crocodiles are aggressive and will strike anybody at any time, and there's nothing he can do about that), which led him to a new thought process involving looking at his fear from an empowering perspective (if he must save his own life, he will do whatever it takes to protect himself).

Feeling determined and courageous leads us to act differently than we do when we are feeling fear; courage gives us the opportunity to create a different result. That new outcome is only possible when we shift our thoughts from an immobilizing belief to a new perspective, and that shift is only possible when we first *acknowledge* the problem, issue, weakness, desire, fear, or whatever else may be holding us back. By doing so, we begin to see what we're really up against, and the power to make actual change then becomes a reality.

My good friend Christine Lavulo, CPSC and fellow life coach, speaker, and trainer shared in her book *Women Who Empower* how she acknowledged her fears, dreams, and desires. It took someone else, however, to help her get the courage to do this since, she explains, it can be very difficult at first to acknowledge these things ourselves. "I was working with a business coach to get my speaking and coaching going, and she took me through some exercises so we could narrow down my core theme. We talked about words that express who I am and the experiences that qualify me for this particular career. It came down to one word…overcomer. I have overcome many obstacles in my life. [But] I never recognized or acknowledged my success over struggle because I didn't think it was 'big enough' to qualify as a real obstacle."

Christine had experienced a teen pregnancy, then a second out of wedlock. She raised two young boys while trying to provide, have a social life, and improve herself. Finally, she found her prince charming and went on to have three more kids but still experienced major financial difficulties. Through all this, she didn't believe her struggles were "big enough" to be considered the backdrop for her coaching. Once she began acknowledging her truth, however, she found a desire to change her story—or at least the way she thought about it. She began to see herself as a person who had truly overcome some pretty significant troubles. She began to see that she did have the power within to put on new words to describe herself, and to think differently about her circumstances, which then gave her the power she needed to pursue her coaching career with passion.

Acknowledging Expands Your World

We've learned that acknowledging can give you the courage to step out of fear and into a life where you can be your truest self. It can also take you out of a constricted, stuck place where you can begin the process of expanding your views and opening yourself to loads of new possibilities. This expanded view helps you not only change the negative beliefs you have been laboring under but also see that you have the capacity already within you to live your best life and become whom you were always meant to be.

Remember my perfectionism? Along with keeping me stuck in a never-ending state of negative discontent, perfectionism also kept me from acknowledging my desire for making a lot more out of my life. I had secret ambitions, but I kept those dreams inside because acknowledging them out loud to another person or even in my prayers to God felt too scary!

One secret desire I had always had but never told anyone was to become a writer and public speaker or broadcast journalist. I remember many nights watching anchors on TV talk shows, nightly news, or even sports reports and dreaming about how that would be me one day. But as soon as the thought came, the negative self-talk began. "Who do you think you are? You don't know how to do that . . . and you never will."

I had fallen into the same kind of constricted, fearful thinking about pursuing my dreams that American YouTuber, comedian, and emotional healing/life coach JP Sears pokes fun at in his satirical video "How to Be More Afraid." With tongue in cheek, he points out what a waste of our life we make when we stay paralyzed by fear instead of pursuing our dreams: "To learn how to be more afraid, always choose a feeling of safety over a feeling of aliveness. Instead of asking the person out, taking the adventure, leaving the job you hate, or doing the thing you've never done before, avoid those dangers so you can keep the pacifier of safety in your mouth . . . because that feels better!"

I also wanted that pacifier of safety in my mouth for a long time, and looking back, it makes sense now that in high school, college, and throughout my life—until I discovered the Word Effect—I never went out on a limb to pursue my dreams. I never took one communication, journalism, or writing class. Perfectionism had such a tight grasp on me that I was too afraid of failing to ever risk pursuing my heart's desires.

My younger sister Kristy, on the other hand, was not afraid to chase after new things and, as a child, took up oil painting and drawing simply because she thought it looked fun. She requested the supplies for Christmas and began to teach herself, watching shows on how to paint and making the attempt. She was willing to create and explore and see what would happen and could laugh at her progress, never seeming to take herself too seriously. She never entertained the idea that perhaps she wasn't any good at creating; she simply *acknowledged* her secret desires and opened herself to lots of new possibilities because of that.

What about you? How many secret desires do you have locked away in your heart that you're too afraid to acknowledge? Are you putting thoughts on such as "I don't have the talent or skill to make my dreams come true," or "She's so much more put together than I am; there's no way I could accomplish what she's done." Are you comparing yourself to others, becoming resentful, judgmental, and defeated? Has the negative set of words you choose to think about yourself become a belief system that keeps you from breaking out of your comfort zone and trying new things?

What if you can start to believe in your future self and not just look back at your past and what you might have always believed about yourself? Master life coach Brook Castillo says this: "Somewhere, typically in our early adulthood, we stop focusing on our future and focus instead on our past to help us decide what we're capable of. We begin choosing thoughts like, 'I've never done it before so I'm not sure I can do it,' 'I've always been overweight; it's just who I am,' or 'I've never been able to lose weight and keep it off.' We limit our future potential based on who we've been and what we've accomplished so far. To focus on our future means we should recognize [acknowledge] limiting beliefs, let them go, and replace them with beliefs that serve our dreams."

I want to encourage you to break out of your confining beliefs by acknowledging that it's all right to have hopes and dreams and that it might even be possible to make them come true! All it takes to do this is to become aware of the kinds of words you are choosing to think about yourself. Are these words positive and light-hearted, like my sister was likely thinking when she took up painting, or are they heavy and defeatist? As I mentioned earlier in this chapter, we often carry with us into adulthood the faulty belief systems we formed as children because we have never stopped to examine what words we are using to think about those beliefs. I invite you to take the challenge at the end of this chapter in order to better understand just what you automatically think about yourself and others and where those words and thoughts ought to be changed.

If you are having trouble being honest with yourself and are not able to admit your fears, worries, dreams, and passions to anyone, I encourage you to really explore the idea of acknowledging what kind of defeatist words you are thinking every day about yourself. Are the words *perfectionism, procrastination,* and *self-pity* commonly coming up in your thought processes? Are these negatively biased words your "friends," the personal dialogue you have become so familiar and comfortable with that you no longer know how to move forward? If so, again, I urge you to consider what acknowledging the words you are thinking might do to start you on the road to a more purpose-driven and fulfilling life.

Everything changed for me when I was able to acknowledge to God that something was wrong and I needed help. As I noted in the Introduction, I was so full of despair and was being choked out of life by my negativity bias that I got on my knees and pleaded for help. I was specific in my prayers and don't ever remember a time when I had opened up to Him with such vulnerability. "Please help me. I need help; something is wrong with me, and I don't know what to do. Every aspect of my life is suffering." That was the beginning of a new life for me, when I really acknowledged my own weakness, admitted

I could not rely on my own strength, and received the impression to change my words.

After taking the leap of faith to acknowledge this truth to my Higher Power, the desire to change began, and I was shown a simple means of making those changes using the power of words. When I opened up to the universe, the universe opened up to me. I didn't have to hide anymore. The scripture found in Matthew 17:20 states, "If ye have faith as a grain of mustard seed, ye shall say unto this mountain, remove hence to yonder place; and it shall remove; and nothing shall be impossible unto you." To have this kind of faith requires nothing more than to acknowledge that you do need this kind of faith as Matthew encourages us!

As I began to discover *how* to change my words, the words would start to find me. I just had to open up to this new idea—acknowledging something was wrong seemed to allow the stars in the universe to line up, and solutions began to appear. The first came as I was watching a Netflix documentary on food, and the following words hit me so strongly that they are all I remember from the film: "Practice saying, 'I accept myself unconditionally right now.'" This idea stuck with me and gave me a little glimmer of hope. *What if this could help me?* I thought. *What if this might make a difference in my life?*

In the beginning, it was hard for me to even remember to say the words at all because I truly did not believe they applied to me. So, I decided to give myself a simple reminder by writing them on an index card and putting the card on my bathroom mirror. I had my doubts about whether anything would come of doing this because in the past, I had posted positive messages around my home in an attempt to think more optimistically about myself. But I had grown accustomed to just walking by those messages, not really absorbing their meaning. They were more a way to make me look the part of being a "good person," but I was not putting them into my heart or mind.

But this time, I tried to approach these words a little differently. Each day while I brushed my teeth in the morning and evening, I would look at those words and practice saying them to myself over and over. I wondered if perhaps this was a way for me to change my words, as God had admonished me to do. What did I have to lose? The negative cycle I had been in for so long threatened to keep me stuck, but as I acknowledged my reality by putting on positive words that didn't even mean anything to me, things began to change. Slowly but surely, I began to step forward into living the life I had always dreamed of.

This shift hasn't been easy, because change requires the consistent and painstakingly slow process of rewiring the brain to ditch bad habits and behaviors and begin to think in a whole new way, but it has certainly been worth the effort. As the old saying goes, "Everything worthwhile takes time." For me, it is something I still work on daily—applying the seven simple Power Words of the Word Effect cycle is a process. That's because the human brain tends to take simple steps and overcomplicate them. The first step is the hardest, but from there it can become easier as we get more familiar with the process. For me, that day I acknowledged where I was and began to explore where I wanted to be gave me the power to begin conceptualizing the ideas found in the Word Effect.

And now, as you put on this first Power Word in the Word Effect, you are learning how to *bridge* your thoughts from where they are to where you want them to be. The Word Effect allows you to get unstuck, to move forward with each day despite the circumstances you are in. You can create the life you desire with the power of words. The Word Effect is the creative process that allows you to start moving forward.

As you stop walking away from your true self and your amazing potential to do and feel good, instead, begin looking up. Reach your hand up to the heavens. You will be met with the hope you need. It all starts when you *acknowledge*.

Before going on to Chapter 3, I'd like to challenge you to face yourself, your weaknesses, your fears, and your deepest desires honestly. As you acknowledge them, you will be filled with hope and have the courage to take steps that cycle upward toward your true potential. As Confucius is purported to have said, "It does not matter how slowly you go so long as you do not stop."

Challenge Your Fears by Being Willing to Acknowledge Your True Potential

1. What is one thing you are afraid to acknowledge? How do you feel about this? Write it down. _____

_____

_____

_____

_____

_____

2. As you figure out your thoughts (and the words you are using to describe them), toss out any that don't really serve you by acknowledging how little they help you. Then decide to think a bit differently.

3. Write down and then post on your mirror the following words: "I accept myself unconditionally, right now." Practice saying them five times in the morning, five times during the day, and five times at night.

4. Commit to the Power Word *acknowledge* until you see things change. There is no timetable for change—we are each on our own path—but this Power Word will work if you work for it.

As you take this challenge, I hope you will catch the same glimmer of hope I did when I finally acknowledged I was afraid to live and just be me. Now join me as we move ahead to the next chapter, where we will explore Power Word two and the importance of "asking."

"Not I, not anyone else can travel that road for you;
you must travel it for yourself."
—Walt Whitman

CHAPTER 3

ASK

THE POWER WORD THAT INSPIRES CURIOSITY AND INVITES CHANGE

"He who is afraid of asking is ashamed of learning."
—Danish Proverb

Power Word 2: *Ask (verb) – to request something in order to obtain an answer or glean new information.*

Have you ever been looking forward to receiving a gift for a special event and built up so much anticipation around receiving it, only to be disappointed upon opening the present? In the past, when I was leading a life of discontent, this was often the place in which I found myself—many times, the reality of what was inside the beautifully wrapped present my family gave me did not meet my expectations. I would anticipate the gift but was never clear on what I wanted in the first place, so I often felt dissatisfied.

Typically, prior to most birthdays, I would give several clues to my husband and kids about what I wanted. But then, when they chose just one item to give me off my "list," instead of feeling gratitude, I would feel somewhat let down because they didn't get me what I truly hoped for. They took my clues and subtle, laid-back approach to mean, "I don't need anything . . . I will be happy with whatever." But even though this was what I seemed to be saying, it definitely wasn't what I meant! I'm not sure how I expected them to know what I really wanted when I myself wasn't even decided on anything at times.

Throughout our marriage, my husband has often repeated to me the old adage, "Say what you mean and mean what you say!" Sounds simple, right? I have realized over the years, however, that this is easier said than done. I have had to pause and really think about that statement. Am I able to say what I mean if I don't even know what that is? Do I mean what I say?

In my efforts to acknowledge who I really am and my true feelings and desires, I have had to become more aware of the words I think and say. After *acknowledging* them (and doing so with more honesty), I have been able to be more vulnerable, and that has led to the natural desire to ask more questions:

- What do I really think about myself?
- How do I truly feel?
- What are my actual priorities?
- What do I value most?
- Why do certain things matter to me?
- Who do I want to become?

As I have asked more and more honest questions like these, I have found great power in the word *ask*. When I have taken the time to look closely at myself by asking the questions that matter most to me, I have finally been able to discover what *my* truths are for *my* life. Author Suzy Kassem in her book, *Rise Up and Salute the Sun: The Writings of Suzy Kassem*, has said, "To seek truth requires one to ask the right questions. . . . Those on the right path of Truth are extremely heart-driven and childlike in their quest, always asking questions, always wanting to understand and know everything and are not afraid to admit they don't know something. . . . If the mind is in the way, the heart won't see anything."

When I have opened up and allowed myself to acknowledge the need to be more vulnerable, become more curious, and ask not only hard questions but genuine questions, my life has changed dramatically over time. As I have become more willing to ask questions, I have let go of my ego, ignorance, and self-centeredness and become a truth seeker. Letting go of the appearance of knowing everything and allowing myself to be a human being who is open to new ideas has been one of the most effective ways to overcome emotional childishness and a bias toward negativity. I have been better able to appreciate the gifts that have been given to me. I have learned how to be less afraid. I have understood myself and others better. I have seen ways to make lasting and significant changes. My perspective on life has completely shifted! Asking keeps my transformation moving forward with momentum, energy, and motivation. That's why *ask* is one of the seven Power Words in the Word Effect cycle of becoming. That's why I now live by this word and want to it share with you.

> *When you consistently* **ask** *needful questions of yourself, your relationships, the world, the universe, and your Higher Power, you open yourself up to so many more possibilities for change and progress than when you choose to hide within your "safe" zone of negativity and discontent.*

Throughout the remainder of this chapter, I want to show you why this statement is true and how asking can lead to further growth and development. As you *acknowledge* your weaknesses, strengths, desires, and passions (putting on Power Word 1), you will naturally be prompted to *ask* questions about those things (putting on Power Word 2). This Power Word will spur you to look more closely at your thoughts and how the words you choose to put on affect those thoughts. This is the power of the Word Effect: the way you use certain words can transform your thinking, which in turn changes your actions and ultimately allows you to create the kind of life you were always meant to live.

Asking Questions Is an Important Catalyst for Change

In the work I do with my life coaching clients, we spend a great deal of time on the power of questions. The certification manual for the Life Coach School states, "Questions reveal thoughts and can also direct us to think new ones. . . . Don't ever underestimate how many of us are on autopilot, playing out the programming of our childhoods without questioning it. We do what we think we should do based on what we were told as children, and we have never evaluated whether it still applies." How often do you think the same set of thoughts over and over again, never stopping to *ask* if you like these thoughts or not? Most people, as they grow older, lose the delightful curiosity of youth and stop questioning things, falling in line with what everyone else is doing. This pattern often leads to looking at life through a muted lens, which usually results in a very warped perspective about who you are and what you want to become.

Perhaps you feel like you are stagnating, that your psyche's growth has been stunted. If you have stopped asking powerful questions because you are just letting your brain operate robotically, thinking the same things (or questions) repeatedly, you are likely falling prey to negativity bias. Negative feelings beget negative thinking and negative questions, and we then get a lot of negative "answers" because we can no longer see the good in anything. Here is an example from the Life Coach School's certification program that illustrates this point:

"If you were to ask a client, 'Why can't you lose weight?' the person will give you all the reasons why they can't lose weight. Alternatively, when you ask a client a positive question, they'll answer with positive thoughts. For example, 'How have you been successful at this?' Or 'How can you enjoy this process?'" Notice that both negative and positive ideas in this example appear in question form, but one starts with "why" and the other with "how."

Great power comes from the questions you ask, so make sure your questions are empowering and not just the same old negative inquiries you may have been making over and over again. Stop asking about how unfair the world is or why your life must be the way it is. Until now, you may not have been aware of the words you have been choosing to think about yourself and your life, and those thoughts include the questions you ask yourself. But now you can apply the Word Effect to change the cycle of negative questions.

As you discover the power of the Word Effect in your own life, it will awaken that old sense of curiosity you had as a child. It will allow you to stay inquisitive, asking meaningful questions, which actually helps focus the mind. The Life Coach Certification Program teaches that "by asking high quality, empowering questions, we get creative and inspiring answers. It's like our brain goes to work searching for the answers to what we're presenting."

As human beings, we ask ourselves questions all day long. You might not realize it now, but asking positive questions has the power to move you forward, while negative questions can do nothing but hold you back. I encourage you to become more aware of the words you are using to form the questions you ask in your mind. Are you phrasing those questions in a negative way with words such as "Why me?" or "What now?" Or are you forming inquiries with positive words like "What can I do?" or "How is this significant?" As you become more aware of the words you put on, you will not only become more conscious of the types of questions you ask yourself but of God and the universe as well.

Albert Einstein once said, "The mind that opens to a new idea never returns to its original size." We all have obstacles come into our lives of all different shapes and sizes, but with every obstacle we acknowledge, we have the power to then ask questions and discover strategies to help us move forward. When I lean into my ego, it keeps me stuck. When I ask questions, I find the answers I need.

Empowering Questions Empower Change

Remember the friend I mentioned in the Introduction who asked me a simple but life-changing question about the way I was approaching all my negative discontent? "Becky, why don't you stop wondering 'why' and start asking 'how' instead?" When I followed her advice, God was able to help me see that change was possible—not through willpower, but through word power. By framing questions positively, such as "How can I change?" instead of "Why is this happening to me?" my life has become so much more beautiful.

This concept is perfectly illustrated by the Life Coach Certification Program: "If you ask yourself, '**Why** can't I lose weight?' you'll come back with a slew of very negative, self-defeating answers. The question incorporates a negative belief, and your brain will be sent to task to prove that negative belief correct." When I work with coaching clients, the first reminder is always our thoughts are optional. Yet for so many of us, we continue to put on those same thoughts of negativity.

Our brain is a very powerful tool, and if not directed toward the good, it looks to what it knows and continues to focus there. In our session, we will first uncover those thoughts and then when the client is ready to explore new thoughts regarding the particular circumstance, we begin to explore and consider them. It is so powerful to see another person realize that the power to change their story is truly within them. Having a front row to guide those who desire to change is one of my greatest blessings. It reminds me of the power of change again and again.

When we begin to change our questions to incorporate an empowering belief, we will begin to come up with answers that empower us forward. For example, the question could be, 'How can I lose weight permanently and have fun at the same time?' [When phrased like this,] you will likely come up with much more creative and wonderful ideas that will move you closer to your goal.

When you empower your brain with empowering questions that have been formed using empowering words, you will discover the steps needed to continue transforming your life—one word at a time. I was able to start changing the direction of my life when I began asking "how" instead of "why" concerning any situation I faced that I didn't appreciate, hadn't planned on, or thought wasn't needed. This simple change of one word made all the difference in the way I approached my feelings, my relationships with others, and how I came before God—asking "how" conditions the brain to seek knowledge and even wisdom while at the same time humbly acknowledging your imperfection.

Admitting You Don't Know All the Answers

Accepting that you need help and don't know everything, however, can be difficult for many of us to do. Here's a case in point: You no doubt have heard the old joke about the husband and wife out driving. When they get lost, the man will not pull over to ask for directions, and the wife becomes furious that he is not following her instructions. I hate to admit it, but I am a lot like the husband in this joke; I struggle to ask for help. I don't want to look silly or foolish because I don't know all the answers. At other times I am very much like the wife in the passenger seat, who seems to have the solution for everything, thinking that I'm able to tell my husband, children, or anyone else that I think they're wrong. It's much easier to tell someone what to do than to look at our own culpability!

Why is this? Why is it so hard for us to admit that we could possibly be wrong or need help? Why is it so difficult to ask for assistance when we're in the driver's seat of life? I have pondered these questions for some time and have concluded that one reason, at least for me, is that I might not want to do whatever is suggested. That sounds silly at first, but think about it . . . Haven't there been times when you have asked for suggestions on how to do something, but when the advice has been given, it has sounded so absurd to you that you wished you hadn't asked in the first place? This has certainly happened to me. But I have learned that if I'm going to ask for anything, I need to check my pride and be willing to just sit with the suggestion for a bit and wait. When I have done this, I have opened myself to other ways of approaching things—and some of them have been absolutely wonderful!

When I begin to feel as if I don't want to ask for help or listen to anyone else's ideas, I return to a story my good friend Bryn shared with me: "Several years ago, our backyard fence broke. It needed to be fixed, and I thought about it and decided the best way to fix it was a particular way." She then shared her enlightened and thoughtful solution to the problem with her husband. He listened, replied with an "Okay," and then said to her, "I think I will do it this way instead."

My friend, of course, became irritated by his disregard; she felt wronged, offended, and resentful that her husband wasn't even going to consider her suggestion. "Didn't he know that I had really thought things through?" she asked herself. "I have come up with the right way!" Bryn despised the entire repair process, and it ultimately caused great contention in their lives. Secretly she hoped the fence might fall down again after her husband's repair job. But here's where the story ends: over ten years have passed since the fence was fixed, and it's still standing and has never been a problem since.

Bryn shared her story with me to help me better understand my own issues with asking, and I was able to learn from her experience. She gave me the opportunity to see that there might be more than one way to do things. Every time I need to make a decision about taking or not taking another person's advice after I have asked for it, this simple thought comes to me: "Remember the fence." Bryn's experience has taught me that I shouldn't hesitate to ask just because I might not get my way.

The power of asking questions and becoming open-minded happens when you reduce your expectations of how you think things should go. The *how* of things unfolds in the doing, not the thinking. The way is often not clear immediately. You start a project, an idea, or even a dream by asking how and being open to the path you go down. The misery sets in when you stop asking for help and push your agenda down the path you think it should go down.

Sometimes I struggle to ask for help because I worry I might give the impression to others that I'm not as intelligent and knowledgeable as I'd like them to think I am. Asking for help feels like a blatant confession of weakness—after all, don't we all want to know all the answers? But if you look back in history, the people who have made the greatest contributions to the world are those who failed and failed but continued to ask for help, to ask questions, to be curious, to be vulnerable, to acknowledge that they didn't know all the answers—and that that was okay. They didn't labor under the prideful delusion that they might look stupid or foolish just because of this fact. Being willing to ask kept them moving forward.

Thomas Edison, described as America's greatest inventor, is such a person. Edison developed and invented many amazing things in his lifetime and the most notable is the light bulb which has had a widespread impact on our world. Yet how many of us have taken Edison for granted in thinking that he just popped into his laboratory one day and tinkered around a bit and did this and that, and ta-da! The light bult was invented! History tells us otherwise.

In his attempts to develop and perfect the incandescent light bulb, Edison failed and failed and failed, over and over again. In fact, he failed close to ten thousand times. We might fume over so many failures, but the famous inventor reacted differently. "Thomas Edison had an extraordinarily positive perception of life that greatly enhanced his ability as an inventor," writes Napoleon Hill in his book *Think and Grow Rich*.

"The great Edison simply viewed each unsuccessful experiment as the elimination of a solution that wouldn't work, thereby moving him that much closer to a successful solution. We could all take a lesson from Edison . . . There are few obstacles in life that will not succumb to consistent, sustained, intelligent, positive action. When you are discouraged after you've failed at something, remember Edison's 10,000 failures before he arrived at the solution that forever changed the world."

Although Edison failed repeatedly, he continued on nonetheless, asking questions of himself and others as to what wasn't working until he found the solution to the problem. He became a truth seeker who let go of his ego, and with each obstacle he encountered, he doggedly worked at a successful outcome. Of his continued "failure" with the light bulb, he has said this of the undertaking: "I have not failed. I've just found 10,000 ways that won't work. . . . Just because something doesn't do what you planned it to do doesn't mean it's useless."

Edison's experience teaches us all that even failures are valuable because they can lead us to better and more helpful questions, which in turn get us closer to the results we are seeking. All his "failures" gave him a chance to keep asking (and remain curious) until he arrived at the place he was supposed to be. If he had succeeded after the third or fourth time of trying, imagine all the discovery, insight, and wisdom he would have missed out on. Perhaps Edison's real success was not so much the invention of the light bulb (and all his other marvelous designs), but in all, he learned about himself and the process of becoming.

In pondering Edison's work, I was led to ask another important question: Is there a solution to all my problems, to all your problems, and to all the world's problems? I have come to believe that the answer to that question is yes, there is a solution to all our problems if we are willing to ask the right questions and become open-minded about new and different ideas—solutions we may have never focused on before.

The scientific method provides another excellent example of the power of asking the right questions. This method starts by asking a question about a particular subject, doing research on that subject, constructing a hypothesis, testing that hypothesis, then asking more questions: Is the procedure working? No? Then change the experiment. Ask more questions: Still not working? Analyze the data and draw conclusions. Create a new hypothesis. Continue this process of asking and adjusting until you gain a reasonable understanding. Reaching this level of comprehension, all starts with asking questions and not giving up until you feel confident in the results.

While I didn't realize the science behind it at the time, the genesis of the Word Effect concept came about as I experimented with ways to become more aware of my words. As I made a conscious effort to change my words and *ask* empowering questions, I came to see that words matter, and their effect on us—the Word Effect—has the power to transform lives for good.

Consistent Curious Inquiry, Followed by Action, Leads to Great Outcomes

One of my favorite quotes of all time is this one by the late Richard G. Scott, an apostle of The Church of Jesus Christ of Latter-day Saints: "Remember, little things lead to big things. Seemingly insignificant indiscretions or neglect can lead to big problems. More importantly, simple, consistent, good habits lead to a life full of bountiful blessings."

I love this quote for many reasons, but in terms of *asking*, it reminds me that the simple and consistent habits of inquiring after wisdom and insight, changing our perspective, and seeking out the right answers can—over time—give solutions to many of our struggles. When you consistently seek, ask, and knock, the way will be opened to you, as the Bible teaches in Matthew 7:7–8:

> *"Ask, and it shall be given you; seek, and ye shall find; knock, and it shall be opened unto you: For every one that asketh receiveth; and he that seeketh findeth; and to him that knocketh it shall be opened."*

But your reward does not just depend alone on seeking and asking. The way forward to creating your most beautiful life and becoming the person you are meant to be requires you to carefully consider the answers you receive to all your questions. It requires you to ponder on them, ask your Higher Power if they are right, and then *act* on those that you know are the truths you are to seek out (which we will talk more about in Chapter 6). I have heard it said before that EGO stands for "edging God out." This might be why I have the hardest time asking God questions and acting on answers—because I'm afraid His way and my way are different.

I want to be in control. Like fixing the fence, I often think my way of doing something is the right way. But when I ask God, He normally has a better way, one that requires faith in order to take the steps needed to follow His way. I learned through an experience with my doctor what happens when we don't act on the answers we receive.

A few years ago, at my annual physical, I began complaining to my doctor about some problems I had been having and the discomfort I was experiencing. As I opened up to him frankly about what was going on, I guess, in some way, I was asking for help. He suggested a procedure he thought I would benefit from, but it was something I was unfamiliar with. This procedure had a few problems, in my mind, including the risk of not being successful, some out-of-pocket expenses, and the possibility of some physical discomfort.

I left the doctor's office that day with additional information, but as I thought about the procedure, I decided to wait. Was there a chance that my problem would go away if I just didn't think about it? It might. "Maybe if I stop asking questions about this, it will just go away," I thought. I could hope so. But as the year progressed, I began to struggle with my physical issue more and more.

A year later, I sat in my doctor's office again and began complaining about my problem once more. He looked at me and said, "I still recommend the procedure. What made you not do it?" I got honest and told him I was worried it might not work. I might be in the statistical five percent for which the procedure wasn't effective. I was worried about the cost because it was a big out-of-pocket expense. Plus, I told him, I feared the pain and discomfort the procedure might cause me. My kind doctor then smiled at me and said some words I will never forget: "You can take the chance and try the procedure, or you can keep complaining about this problem for the next ten years."

Somehow those words at that moment penetrated my heart and mind. It was my choice! My doctor had given me his expertise and advice, but the decision was up to me. The power to take action was within me and had been all along. I went home and decided right then and there that I was going to move forward with the procedure. I called my doctor's office to find out what I needed to do next, asking more and more questions as I went along. With each question came another answer or suggestion, and the way opened up for me to feel good about having the procedure, along with a way to pay for it.

In a few months, I was ready for and had scheduled the procedure, and guess what? It worked! While the discomfort was there for a few days, it was quickly forgotten. Having that procedure was one of the best decisions I have ever made. Besides fixing the medical problem itself, it has also improved my quality of life tenfold. My doctor's simple words opened the door to further inquiry and consistent follow-through on the answers and suggestions I received from reaching out for help.

Wow! Did I learn a valuable lesson about how important it is to *take action after asking for help*. When we remain curious and keep asking questions, the path we need to take will become clearer because often, the answer is not just one answer but a series of discoveries that propel us forward.

The Word Effect perfectly illustrates how the cycle of Power Words carries us forward and gives us the strength to continue moving along the path of self-discovery and self-mastery. When you first *acknowledge* where you are and what you want, you naturally begin to *ask* questions—you stay curious. As you take steps forward and act on the answers to your questions, the path you need to be on will become clearer. That clarity comes by taking steps and asking questions.

It takes faith and courage to ask and then keep asking—to remain curious. Sometimes you might start down one path and find that it leads to a dead end. This doesn't mean you did something wrong. In fact, sometimes you may learn more from taking the wrong path than you will from heading in the right direction. I love what Albert Einstein has said about being persistent in our efforts to learn and grow, even when we sometimes wander in the wrong direction: "The important thing is not to stop questioning. Curiosity has its own reason for existing." Once you've learned your lesson, you shouldn't linger on the path, berating yourself for making a wrong choice and languishing in your mistakes. Back up! As soon as you realize it's time to start down a different path, simply turn around and try again.

Awaken Your Sense of Curiosity Using the "HOW" Process

My fear of asking questions, as I explained earlier, was largely because I was afraid of the answers I might get, that the answer might be "no." But the fact is, the answer is automatically "no" if you never ask. Hopefully, you know by now that there are no wrong questions. The only wrong questions are the ones not asked. I love what Steve Jobs said about this: "Most people never ask, that's what separates the people that do things from the people that just dream about them." I have tried to teach my kids this principle, even though in the past, I believed it was truer for them than it was for me. I think it is often easier to suggest to others to stay curious but to live our own lives like this brings uncertainty that we often try to avoid.

One way I learned to stop being afraid of asking and to remain more curious was within a twelve-step recovery program, where I was encouraged to say "how" more often in the way I framed my questions. This word has not only helped me with the addiction issues I struggle with but has proven helpful in every area of my life. Words are so powerful that once you learn how to use them for one situation, you can use them in many others as well. Each new problem, each new life circumstance, can be directed by the right set of words. Each day as I strive to put on the Word Effect's Power Words, I open myself up to what I like to call the "HOW" process for asking questions and solving problems:

> **H** – Honesty: Be honest with yourself and acknowledge you may not know the next step.
>
> **O** – Open-mindedness: Be willing to hear and entertain new ideas.
>
> **W** – Willingness: Have the desire to act on those new ideas, try new things, and put in place new approaches to life.

The idea surrounding this process came from a mentor of mine from a twelve-step program, who gave me the suggestion to approach my questions using *honesty, open-mindedness,* and a *willingness* to try applying my answers. She explained to me that many problems, choices, and situations we face in life are not "black and white" and that this stiff, inflexible "right and wrong" thinking precludes us from an entire universe of wisdom, understanding, and beauty. We start to see the good in the universe by honestly and openly asking and then being willing to act on the answers we receive. Applying the HOW process changes a constricted view of life by helping us see these truths:

- We may not have come up with the right solution yet, but we can continue looking for guidance.
- We can benefit from looking at things from more than one angle.
- We must be willing to act on new perspectives if we ever hope to harness the magnificent power of the universe and all it holds for us.

At first, I resisted my mentor's suggestion to approach life this way, but one day, after some time avoiding the idea, I decided to give the

HOW process a try. I was about to turn forty and my life had hit rock bottom, as I have explained in previous chapters. I didn't really see then that I had dug myself into a big pit of negativity and that I was struggling to see any light and goodness in the world. Reacting as an emotional child focused my steps and gaze downward, and this negativity continued to grow stronger each day.

Marie Forleo, author of *Everything is Figureoutable*, explains that she had feelings very similar to mine at one point in her life. While our stories aren't exactly the same, what we do have in common were feelings of discontent. Our circumstances were different, but the thoughts and feelings we were having are similar.

"I felt like a total failure," Marie recalls in her book. "Less than a year earlier, I'd graduated the valedictorian of Seton Hall University. Yet here I was sitting on the steps of Trinity Church in lower Manhattan, in tears." She had graduated, gotten the job, and done all the right things—or at least what she thought were the right things—to please everyone else, and she still didn't feel happy."

As a trading assistant on the floor of the New York Stock exchange on Wall Street, I had pride, a steady paycheck, and health insurance. I was grateful to have a job, but inside I felt like I was dying. This little voice inside me kept whispering . . . this isn't where you're supposed to be. This isn't what you're supposed to be doing with your life." At my lowest point, I could certainly relate to Marie's experience. My life wasn't what I wanted it to be.

Like me, Marie tried to push aside her worries, but they kept pressing on her. One day at work, her stress mounted so severely that she felt physically ill and had to run outside to get some air. She ran to the nearest church building and began praying, asking what was wrong with her.

"Why can't I stop these voices in my head? If it's You telling me to quit, can You please tell me what exactly I'm supposed to do instead?! It's not like I have a backup plan. Throw me a sign. I'm dying down here! After a few minutes of pray-crying, I got my first clue on what to do next, 'Call your dad.'"

Marie goes on to share how she went from asking "why" to taking the next step to call her dad, as well as what transpired in her life as she continued to ask questions in the HOW way. She started being *honest* with where she was, *open* about possible solutions, and *willing* to take action when the time was right. While the road to creating an authentically beautiful life wasn't easy, once she started asking empowering questions, she was able to move forward. And the direction to take became clearer with every step she took.

On her journey of becoming whom she was meant to be, Marie says, "I stumbled across an article about a brand-new profession, 'coaching' (this was the late 1990s—it was all so new back then) . . . [and] when I read the article . . . something inside me lit up. . . . A deep, gentle presence inside me said, 'This is who you are. This is who you're meant to be.'" Marie's struggle wasn't over then, and she experienced so much self-doubt and criticism from every corner of her life, telling her she was stupid. But that voice in her head gave her the courage to move forward.

She went on to become a leading expert in the life coaching industry and a thought leader (as she has been called by Oprah Winfrey). Now she has her own award-winning television show. From Marie's life, you can see how powerful asking is, and when you bring a Higher Power into it, there's no stopping you.

I share her story because, in many ways, I feel her discontent, unsettled, and unfulfilled feelings paralleled mine. Some of the negative words Marie used to describe her life were words I was using too. And just like her, I had been taught as a little girl to turn to God for answers. As a member of The Church of Jesus Christ of Latter-day Saints, I learned that God loves me and I can ask Him about anything. I was taught that my Heavenly Father wants me to experience joy not only in moments of desperation but in all things, big or small. I learned I could ask Him for help, and He will hear my prayers and bless me with knowing the next steps I need to take.

Once I had my own children, I taught them the same principles. But as I explained earlier, there was a point in my life when I had been spiraling downward in a cycle of discontent, negativity, and self-pity for so long; my prayers were no longer filled with faith. It wasn't until a series of events I mentioned in the Introduction that I began to feel the need to pour my soul out to my Heavenly Father for real answers.

One day a scripture from the Bible, which I was very familiar with and had read many times before, caught my attention:

> *"If any of you lack wisdom, let him ask of God, that giveth to all men [and I will insert women] liberally, and upbraideth not; and it shall be given him [or her]" (James 1:5).*

This time when reading these words, I had an immediate desire to put them on myself. I lacked such wisdom in my life that I knew I wanted to ask God for help with an earnestness I had never prayed with before.

I started out by saying, "Father, I believe in you, but for some time, I have felt very alone and by myself. I am here to ask for help and am willing to do whatever you put before me." As you'll remember, He then prompted me to "change [my] words," leading me to discover the Word Effect and how the seven Power Words would mold me and create the life story I desired.

After asking for help, things didn't change for me overnight. I questioned whether I was willing to practice using new words to change my thoughts and, consequently, my whole approach to life. Changing the words that make up your thoughts can be equated to trying to get your muscles back in shape after letting them become weak and flabby. Initially, it can be really hard to get to the gym that first day you decide to "get in shape." Even after buying new shoes, wearing cute workout clothes, and getting a membership, going to the gym can still be hard.

There are always reasons not to go. "I don't feel like it. I'm tired. I have something else to do with my time that seems more important." Of course, I'm sure you've noticed that when you do get back to working out, it feels good, and you have a sense of accomplishment after making the effort—you work your biceps and triceps, you work your hamstrings and quads, and you feel proud. "I did it!" you say to yourself.

But the next day, you wake up really sore, and the following day you feel even worse. Perhaps you look in the mirror and see no immediate changes, and disappointment kicks in. You don't like to feel sore. You don't like the discomfort. But as you remain consistent with putting your shoes on and getting to the gym, working out gets easier over time. It becomes your routine. You commit to going, and the soreness goes away. You begin to feel stronger, happier, and more confident.

Strengthening yourself emotionally by changing the words you think every day is just like getting in shape physically—only harder in the beginning. It can be difficult at first to see any changes on the inside. But transforming internally is just like getting in shape physically: it takes time and consistent behavior to recognize that things are improving, life is getting better, and you are getting stronger.

I am still learning how to take those consistent steps toward improvement, to work through the cycle of Power Words in each new situation and with each new challenge that arises. I still have to remind myself to ask the right questions using the "HOW" process. It takes time and consistent practice. And just when you think you might be getting the hang of things, when you have learned to ask "how" instead of "why," a new set of obstacles seem to crop up. My friend, Kira, a successful art consulting entrepreneur, told me once, "Just when you get one question answered, you find you now have ten more questions to figure out!" There will always be questions, so I invite you to discover the importance of asking.

Over time I have learned to ask myself what words I want to put on each day to bring me closer to the solutions I am seeking. When I circle back to *acknowledge* my doubts, fears, and weaknesses, then apply the "HOW" process (honesty, open-mindedness, and willingness), I always find new and sometimes completely surprising ways of dealing with each new challenge that comes along. Answers and opportunities for change seem to come line upon line, step by step. Each new piece of knowledge, each new bit of understanding, gives me the strength to propel myself forward, to take consistent action. Applying the HOW process has helped me remain curious and given me the courage to continue asking questions. It has also empowered me to focus on solutions rather than obstacles.

I am here to tell you that you can experience this same life-changing empowerment by applying the Word Effect by first *acknowledging* where you are, then cultivating a curiosity to learn more by consistently *asking* the most needful questions—to become a truth seeker, one small step at a time.

Be Curious about What Others Might Know

It's a beautiful thing to recognize that none of us here on earth need live life alone. We were given to each other in order to help each other. Reflecting on my journey, I see that not only has my loving Heavenly Father been in my life, but also other needed people have been sent my way, my husband is one of the most important. Others include parents, siblings, sponsors, mentors, coaches, and old friends (as well as new) who have come into my life at the exact time I needed them to help me in my progress. I believe there are more who will come into my life as I am ready for them.

Isn't it awesome that we all don't have a bad day at the same time? When I struggle and reach out to others, someone is always willing to listen, and if I ask for help, maybe I will even be offered a suggestion or two that I might need to hear from them. And as I am able, I can help those who need my particular care. Remember, we are more similar than different, and we all need each other!

And, of course, God is always there, waiting for you to ask for help. It might be uncomfortable at first, but over time you can learn to exercise your spiritual "asking muscles" more consistently. As I learned to ask more conscientiously, my life began to change. I now practice asking God daily about those things I need particular help with, and when I forget, which I do many times because it is my nature to try to do things on my own, I am gently reminded that I must stay open and vulnerable in order to continue progressing. While writing this book, I began each chapter with a prayer, asking God to speak through me, to help me convey the simple message that has been placed upon my heart, and I believe He has answered those prayers.

When things get hard and I start to spin in circles in my head, I take a minute to acknowledge the power of the word *ask*. The consistent habit of asking has gotten me where I am today. So, I keep on asking, and for this, I have been given in return a life full of bountiful blessings. Being able to see how important this word is and to put it on as part of the Word Effect can be one of the greatest blessings of your life as well.

I am still on my journey of becoming and believe I always will be, but as I look back on how far I've come, I realize that by staying curious, asking simple questions, being willing to accept answers with an open heart, and then acting upon them willingly and consistently, I have been able to free myself of my negativity bias, open myself to new ways of thinking about my circumstances, and take action in ways that have completely changed my life.

To conclude this chapter, I challenge you to let go of your pride and be more willing to be vulnerable by *asking* questions. Become curious about where your life is headed and ask if the story you are living is the one you desire to live. I encourage you to take the following challenge before moving on to the next Power Word (*accept*), which we will explore in Chapter 4.

Challenge Your Ego by Getting Curious and Having the Courage to Ask the Right Questions

1. "HOW" will you step forward into more curiosity so you can make the desired changes to your life?

    a) **H:** *Honestly* write down something you want to change. ___
    _____
    _____

    b) **O:** Become *open* to the words you will need to think or put on to make this change (and write the words here). _____
    _____
    _____

    c) **W:** How will you remain *willing* to ask for help to make this change and allow the process to happen as it will? _____
    _____
    _____

2. Consider asking yourself every day the following superlative questions as found in The Life Coach Certification Program:

    - How can I be an example of what's possible?
    - What can I do to laugh more today?
    - How can I make today better than yesterday?
    - How can I make my future more exciting than my past?
    - How can I make myself a priority so I have more to give others?
    - What do I love about myself?
    - What am I grateful for?
    - How can I honor my body today?

- What can I do to feel my emotions instead of eating them today?
- How can I become more connected to my internal joy?
- How can I make choices that benefit me and everyone around me at the same time?
- How can I live my best life?

Answer one question a day. Since there are twelve, my suggestion is to write down the question, then allow yourself time to really answer it. Don't edit yourself—there is no one grading you. After about two weeks of answering these questions, go back and review your answers to see if they have become new beliefs, you can start accepting as part of who you are.

"One who never asks either knows everything or nothing."
—Malcom Forbes

CHAPTER 4

ACCEPT

THE KEY TO GREATER GROWTH AND PERSONAL DEVELOPMENT

"You must take personal responsibility.
You cannot change the circumstances, the seasons,
or the wind, but you can change yourself.
That is something you have charge of."
—Jim Rohn

Power Word 3: *Accept (verb) – the action of consenting to receive or undertake something offered.*

For many years as an adult, I tried to balance my life as if I were perched on a one-legged stool, completely off-kilter and teetering on the verge of collapse. In my discontent life (before I discovered the power of the Word Effect), I was totally off balance, blaming my problems on my personal circumstances: "If only my husband made more money and we had more financial security, then I would be okay," or "If my kids behaved a certain way, then that would help me feel peace," or "If only I was a little taller, skinnier, smarter, kinder . . ." These feelings of dissatisfaction—of living in the "if only"—made me feel as if I were sitting on a one-legged stool. All the negative thinking allowed my brain to keep looking for more evidence of all the things I didn't have control over, leading me to believe my feelings of instability came from my circumstances and external conditions and not from within myself. I wasn't able to *accept* my life for what it was—instead, I was waiting for life to change. I wanted everyone and everything else to shift and didn't realize I needed to look at changing myself first.

As I continued to sit on my one-legged stool, it became impossible to keep my balance—after all, doing the same things over and over while expecting a different result is a definition of insanity as Albert Einstein is credited with saying. Because I felt powerless to change, I continued to put on thoughts that subconsciously developed my personality to be more discontent and controlling. The Power Word *accept* was as far from my internal vocabulary as I could get and almost impossible to put on. I couldn't accept *anything* about my life!

Even as I tried to sit on one leg, I would seek to control my external circumstances by leaning forward to suggest how others might need to change. But while trying to manage everyone else, I would invariably lose control of myself. When off balance, I had thoughts that left me feeling frustrated, angry, discontent, and resentful—all negative emotions that only perpetuated the insanity.

When we want to change others because we can't accept aspects of our own life, we often find ourselves in the "compare and despair game." Theodore Roosevelt was known to say, "Comparison is the thief of joy," and Mark Twain once remarked, "Comparison is the death of joy." We take our worst day and compare it to the storybook version of someone else's "best day," and then we begin thinking negative thoughts of dissatisfaction and discontent over and over again. Those thoughts become beliefs and we stop questioning them, assuming our life is unacceptable since it doesn't seem to stack up to everyone else's.

If, like I was, you are attempting to balance on a one-legged stool as you try to change your external circumstances instead of accepting your own life as it is right now, you are likely feeling very off-kilter and devoid of joy! This approach to living is probably preventing you from progressing toward creating the beautiful life you are meant to lead. It certainly caused problems for me as the more I tried to change others, the more off-balance and out of whack I became.

Getting off my one-legged stool required that I *accept* my circumstances as they were and not focus on everything or everyone around me. As I began applying the Word Effect, I learned just how important and useful it is to be firmly planted on the ground and that a sturdy, stable approach to living comes from accepting myself where I am in the moment.

*When you **accept**, you live life in the present. It allows you to be content with "what is" rather than waiting on "what if." It encourages you to take personal responsibility for that over which you have actual control and opens the way to choosing happiness.*

Throughout the remainder of this chapter, I want to show you why these thoughts have value and how *acceptance* can be an important guide to further growth and development. Keep in mind that although *acceptance* may seem nearly identical to the Power Word *acknowledge*, these words are distinct in an important way. When we *acknowledge*, we admit to ourselves that we are imperfect and need to change by first changing our mindset or our words. When we *accept*, we let go of the idea that we need to be perfect *now* and can instead move forward with the strengths and weaknesses we currently have. *Acknowledging* sets us on the path of change, and *acceptance* keeps us from getting overwhelmed and discouraged on that path.

As I explained in the Introduction, many of us must be careful to monitor our thoughts (the words we use) because they will easily become beliefs. You and I can become a "watcher" of our own thoughts, as life coach Brooke Castillo teaches. To become a watcher of your own thoughts, you must first *acknowledge* your weaknesses, strengths, desires, and passions (Power Word 1; see Chapter 2). This will naturally prompt you to *ask* questions about those things (Power Word 2; see Chapter 3), which will then spur you to look more closely at your thoughts and how your words affect those thoughts. This process reflects the power of the Word Effect: certain words can transform your thinking, which in turn changes your actions and ultimately allow you to become your most beautiful self.

As you move through this chapter, I want to show you what you can do to achieve greater balance, peace, and joy in your life through some of my own experiences and the stories of others. I want to demonstrate that you can bring more hope, energy, and optimism into your life as you learn how to apply the Power Word *accept*, regardless of what issues you are facing, how off-kilter you feel right now, or what dreams you feel powerless to bring to fruition.

When you begin to focus on what you can control and show up to life differently, you will open yourself to so many wonderful opportunities to become through the Word Effect than you would be trying to perch precariously on the one-legged stool of negative thinking. *Accepting* will allow you to become an even more determined seeker of truth and discover whom you are truly meant to be.

Accepting Lets You Focus on the Right Things

Learning how to accept yourself and your circumstances is one of the most important things you can do to bring balance and beauty into your life. When you accept your present self, you focus less attention on those things that perhaps you fear, hate, or seek to control and open yourself to an expansive universe of love and light. When you can't accept yourself (and others) for who you (or they) really are—warts and all—you close yourself off to all that God wants to bless you with. To be accepting is to be open, vulnerable, willing, and flexible. When you focus on the negative you are resistant, guarded, and restrained. This fearful, dishonest stance can cause you to resist looking at yourself and your internal struggles, trying instead to "fix" others and/or external situations in order to feel better about yourself. But as I mentioned earlier, this practice will keep you stuck and off balance.

Accepting allows you to stop looking outwardly at perceived problems and start focusing inwardly on your potential. I like what author Eric Bjarnson has said about acceptance: "Acceptance is surrendering resistance to God, self, others, and all aspects of life on earth and opening up your heart to receive all the blessings and learning opportunities the Lord is continually showering down upon you." This inward focus has to do with the set of words you choose to think about your life and everything in it. So many distractions in the world today, including our own thought processes, keep us focused on the wrong things. Remember, the words you put on each day can affect the way you feel and act, which ultimately determines your results. Choosing to put on negative words places focus on your *circumstances*. In reality, circumstances are neutral, and the power to change your quality of life is based on your changing your thoughts about your circumstances.

I have seen the truth of this principle played out in my life over and over again. When I truly *accept*, I change my focus from a resistant "what if" perspective to an accepting one of "what is." This shift in focus has changed my life for the better, and my experience is even backed up by science. Tobias van Schneider explains how our brains help us focus on the reality we've accepted. In his article entitled "If You Want It You Might Get It—The Reticular Activating System Explained," van Schneider states, "The Reticular Activating System (RAS) is a bundle of nerves at our brainstem that filters out unnecessary information so the important stuff gets through. The RAS is the reason you learn a new word and then start hearing it everywhere. . . . Your RAS takes what you focus on and creates a filter for it. . . . The RAS seeks information that validates your beliefs."

Our brain has a powerful ability to focus on that which we perceive as important. That is why when you notice a new make and model of a car you like, for instance, you begin to see that car more and more on the roads. If you think you are fat, you might review that idea over and over again when you look in the mirror. Your brain then goes out to gather evidence to prove that what you are thinking is true. Your thoughts determine what you focus on. If you constantly resist who and where you are now, your brain has no room to find satisfaction. Your focus narrows to only the bad you perceive about any given situation. But if you accept your current circumstances, suddenly, your brain can focus on not only the good in those circumstances but also, how you can actively improve your life to find more and more good.

For example, if you believe and think repeatedly something like, "I'm not good enough at this," then you'll almost always notice your failures instead of your successes. But if you accept your shortcomings *and* your strengths, you might think something else instead: "I want to improve at this, and I can if I work hard." Then you'll see your improvement and hard work all the time! The Reticular Activating System explains how the Word Effect can influence your actions, which then affect the kind of life you ultimately get to lead.

So where is your focus? Your brain is like a computer processor of information. It processes what you put in it. The great thing is that you are in charge of your processor. If you don't like the results you are creating, you can *acknowledge* this, *ask* for more understanding, and come to a point where you are better able to *accept* your life as it is right now. Once you stop resisting your circumstances, you will begin to experience the "flow" of the Word Effect, which can ultimately lead you to a place where you can become your true self. This simple confidence in your present self is a powerful tool that allows you to direct your brain.

As you shift your focus, your brain will naturally begin to look for new and better things that will allow you to create your beautiful life.

Accepting Gives You the Courage to Take Personal Responsibility

One of the best ways you can accept your current life is by taking more personal responsibility. "You are 100 percent responsible for your life," Marie Forleo boldly claims in her bestselling book *Everything if Figureoutable*. This is an idea I never considered before I began living the Word Effect. My focus was on what I didn't have control over, and as much as I tried to change those things, I always fell short. My thoughts revolved around such words as "Help me and change them," and of course, those words never worked—they never changed anything about others and ultimately made me feel worse over time. Forleo goes on to share this simple yet mind-blowing idea about focusing on what we are personally responsible for before placing blame for our troubles on any other source. She calls this idea an "essential universal principle":

> Always and in all ways, it's not your parents. It's not the economy. It's not your husband, or your wife, or your family. It's not your boss. It's not the schools you went to. It's not the government or society or institution or your age. You are responsible for what you believe, how you feel and how you behave. To be clear, I'm not saying you're responsible for the actions of others or injustices that have happened to you—but you are responsible for how you respond to the actions of others. In fact, lasting happiness can only come when you take 100 percent responsibility for yourself.

What?! I am *completely* responsible for myself? How can no one else be accountable for my life and happiness? Before I started *acknowledging* my words and *asking* the right questions about my life, it never occurred to me to *accept* that I controlled my life and no one else had the power to change me but *me*! Up until that point, I didn't even know what would make me happy, and I focused all my energy on what was wrong with everything externally instead of what I could control internally.

But now the questions arose: How do I become responsible for what I believe, how I feel, how I show up, and ultimately how I create results? How will shifting my perspective inward make it possible to change me and clean everything else up? These were all questions that spun around in my mind as I began looking at things from a more accepting point of view. As I *asked* "how" and began to explore all these possibilities, I started to see the truth about my own life and that the power to *accept* that life—right as it was in that moment—was one that was in me all along. It was my responsibility to run my life, and I was the only one keeping myself from doing that.

When you accept your life and begin taking personal responsibility, you, too, will stop fighting yourself. The one-legged stool you are teetering on will become more balanced as different words come into your life (remember the RAS). A willingness to submit to and accept the natural flow of life will enter your soul. It may seem like letting go of this "control" would make your life more miserable, but in reality, letting go of the things you cannot change and taking personal responsibility for the things you *can* change make you far happier and more productive.

The day-to-day unfolding of the power found in words will often seem insignificant and uneventful to you, but I'm confident you will find, as I have, that these subtle changes in your thought processes will make all the difference in the world. As my favorite quote by Richard G. Scott asserts, "Little things lead to big things." The Power Word *accept* may seem like such a little thing, but over time it will prove to be a big word that allows you to see the world differently and sit with life in a more balanced way so you can become the person you are meant to be.

Mother Teresa, a Christian nun and missionary who devoted her life to caring for the sick and poor, is known for saying: "Be faithful in small things because it is in them that your strength lies." Thinking accepting words is where your strength will develop, and it will bring subtle changes to your life over time. Your stuck, resistant, and guarded feelings will begin to "flow" away, and you will naturally step forward, little by little, into a place of open, expansive light and energy—and most importantly, to a place of hope.

As I stopped blaming my circumstances for all my trouble and started taking personal responsibility, I naturally and willingly allowed myself to accept some things I had never openly admitted about my life, one of which was a food addiction. My personal tendencies toward hyperfocus didn't help this matter very much. I would zero in on my obsession with food and everything about it that I wasn't doing right, forgetting how important all the other things in my life were. I would commit to my physical improvement, and it was all I thought about. That one leg of my stool was all I had to balance on. For example, when I would get discouraged with my body image, I would decide to go on a diet and really "work" on it. I would show up day after day and do the same workout class at the gym, yet never see any result. Over time I would eventually eat more of something I shouldn't or go days without working out and decide to quit. Quitting on myself became easier than working on me!

After teetering on my stool and not seeing much improvement with my physical obsessions, I would switch my focus and work almost entirely on my mental state. I would rush out to buy some self-help books and commit to doing whatever it took to change my emotional condition. I would start strong, but initiating new ventures is not the hard part for me; it's the consistent efforts over time that have proved difficult. After a few days of working on my mind and thinking, "This is just what I need, this will do the trick," something would come up to sidetrack me, knocking me off my one-legged stool. My attention span was small, and my impatience with myself and others was growing.

After failing to approach physical and mental improvements with any long-lasting integrity, I would then decide that things would get better if I only had a better spiritual connection with God—then I could accomplish what I desired. So, I would knuckle down on everything spiritual, doing the same thing to myself as I had before with my physical and mental zeal. I would commit to making big changes but, over time could not find the balance on this leg either. Yet on the outside, if you asked me how I was doing, I would have told you, "I am doing just fine."

Again, I didn't know how to acknowledge that I was struggling, to ask for help, and especially to *accept* this struggle as a part of my story. It wasn't until I was willing to honestly admit that I had a problem with the way I felt about and dealt with food that I was able to start changing. The Word Effect taught me that the negative words I was choosing to think about food and body image were preventing me from making any real, long-term shifts in my behavior.

I was finally directed to a twelve-step recovery program, where initially, I resisted the idea that I actually needed to participate. But secretly, food and body image had always taken up most of my brain power. I was always thinking of what I should and shouldn't eat. I was constantly trying to stop eating a particular food that I knew wasn't good for me but then continued to indulge and suffer with intense regret for my choices. I went through this cycle again and again. Because eating is a part of daily existence, I never considered that I might have a serious problem with it. In simple terms, I treat food like an alcoholic treats alcohol. I was on a hamster wheel to change my behavior with food, but all I knew was the "diet" and "intense workout" mentality. As hard as I tried, I never found a way to balance the need to eat with how to eat properly, constantly falling off my one-legged stool.

When I finally acknowledged my food addiction and asked God what to do about it, He brought the twelve-step recovery strategy into my life. Because I had *accepted* my current state of living with a food addiction, my brain focused on the words "twelve-step," and I took personal responsibility by admitting that I needed help through a recovery program. I wasn't looking for such a solution, or at least I didn't know I was looking for it, but I remember thinking, "What if this would help me discover and live a more balanced way of life?" Though my brain was shouting that I should quit, I knew I had nothing to lose and so much to gain, and I began feeling a hope I had not experienced for many, many years. I think subconsciously my spirit was craving balance, and I felt encouraged that this 12-step recovery program might be what could give it to me. It was a simple solution, not easy at first to change my way of thinking but it was something I could do with the power of God. This just felt different and there was a ray of hope to give it a try!

As I *acknowledged*, *asked*, and then began to *accept* my story for being exactly that—my story—an amazing shift began to take place. I felt the debilitating inertia of negativity fall away from me bit by bit. Light and energy filled me more than they had in a long time, and I felt like I could finally move forward again. As I continued to look for truth by putting on these Power Words, other amazing ideas began to come into my life—ideas such as the fact that our thoughts create our results.

The Power Word *accept* gives you the courage you need to do this hard work and withstand all the discomfort of stretching beyond your current capacity. It helps you become more willing to try something you haven't done in the past because you will no longer look to your past to give you evidence of what you cannot do. Instead, you will find yourself looking to the future and all the possibilities ahead of what you *can* do. As you *accept* your story as it is today, you can begin anew each day to create the future you have always desired. You can choose to practice putting on different words than those familiar ones you have put on over and over again that have created the same results. You choose to do something different. When you *accept*, you take personal responsibility for the words you choose today, making it possible to look toward your future self—the person you desire to become.

Accepting Is Key to Stepping Forward

How often do you feel a nudge to do something different but then continue to do the same thing? I think this is a natural reaction—part of our human experience. But discovering how to *accept* will prove to be a catalyst that can get you moving forward again.

Sometimes we are held back by fear, especially fear of feeling our emotions. Understanding what feelings are, can help us accept them so we can move forward, and Brooke Castillo explains why in her article "Why Feelings Matter": "A feeling, also an emotion, is a vibration in your body. Nothing more. Without exception, feelings come from our thoughts. They don't 'happen' to us. We create them with our thoughts . . . Feelings always follow thoughts and never the other way around."

If feelings are simply vibrations in the body, as Brooke explains, why are we often afraid to feel our feelings? If they are caused by nothing more than our thoughts and can't hurt us, why do we sometimes resist and avoid feelings at all costs? Because we don't want to deal with the discomfort we perceive will be required to handle the difficult, fearful, or worrisome problems we associate with such feelings. It is only when we begin to *accept* our feelings and lean into the discomfort that we can finally stop perceiving the issues in our life as problems. Instead, we can put forth the effort to change the words that form our thoughts and recognize our problems as opportunities for growth and development. When you change your words, you will change your thoughts, which will allow you to accept your feelings, which will in turn, make it possible for you to face problems and opportunities with courage and even joy. This is how *accepting* helps you step forward again and again into a place of positive energy where you are able to deal with life, accomplish the desires of your heart, and become your best self.

My son Tyler is a great example of accepting life as it is given to him. He takes charge of his thought processes regarding his circumstances, thereby changing the way he feels about what happens in his life. His *acceptance* has been the key to his forward progression and, ultimately his state of happiness.

In high school, Tyler played baseball for a school in Utah that was known for competing for the state championship each year. At the beginning of his senior year, Tyler was working as hard as he could to obtain a starting role—playing second base. Right before the regular season began, the team and families headed to California for a preseason tournament, which didn't go as planned when the varsity team lost six out of six games. As the team met to discuss the tournament, the coaches announced they had decided who would be on the starting team for the regular season. Tyler had made it onto that starting team, playing second base. That evening, despite the sadness of losing and the team not performing the way they had hoped, Tyler was looking forward to the regular season ahead. He was happy his hard work had been noticed and that he was getting the opportunity he had been dreaming about.

The following week when Tyler showed up for the first region game, he noticed that his name had not been posted to play second base. To his surprise, another kid's name was listed with no explanation. That night when he came home, he wasn't ready to talk about the sudden change. When we asked him what happened, all he could say was, "I don't know!"

Tyler found himself in a difficult spot that year as all his other buddies took the field, and he stood there, wondering why he didn't get to join them. Good team players under these particular coaches knew they should never question or ask why a particular decision had been made—like it or not; they were just expected to accept what was and not worry about "what if." No one ever said anything to him like, "Hey Tyler, we changed our mind," or "We decided to try this other kid." Not knowing the reason and trying to fill in the story only brought negativity, sadness, regret, and anger. Tyler felt he could do very little in the circumstance he found himself in.

The season continued and Tyler spent little time on the field, but he was a fast runner. He was given the opportunity to run for the catcher or pitcher as a speed-up runner. He struggled to stay committed in the beginning and to keep showing up because he didn't want to just be a runner. He wanted to play second base! Then he made the decision to be the best team player he could, and this made all the difference in the way he felt about himself and playing baseball. He began accepting his role as a runner, though it wasn't what he wanted or even thought was fair. Tyler embraced his story the best he could and went on to play a valuable and recognizable role in the team, which won the 6A state championship that year.

Part of the team's success was the use of a team mantra: "Whatever It Takes." These words helped them get through the ups and downs of the season. Any spectator who followed the team knew that Tyler had chosen to put those words on intentionally and do his best with what life gave him. At the end of the season, Tyler took pride in knowing that his genuine efforts had contributed to his team's taking the state championship.

While you don't have control over every circumstance in your life, you do have control over what words you choose to think about them. Words of *acceptance* open you to more possibilities for growth and influence. Tyler showed this in his senior year of baseball by choosing affirming words (his team's mantra), which then affected his thoughts. His thoughts, instead of focusing on his disappointing circumstances, allowed him to stay committed to the team goal and to progress and grow. His thoughts, words, and *acceptance* affected the final outcome.

After Tyler's high school graduation, he and I had the opportunity to listen to Chad Hymas, a National Hall of Fame Speaker, address an audience at a National Speakers Association meeting. In that speech, Chad cemented into both of us the idea of *acceptance* being the key to our ability to move forward.

On April 3, 2001, Chad's life instantly changed when a one-ton bale of hay fell on him and broke his neck. From that minute, he became a quadriplegic, paralyzed from the chest down with limited use of his arms and legs. He became wheelchair-bound and had to rely on others to meet all his needs, from bathing to dressing, to brushing his teeth . . . everything.

After this unthinkable accident, Chad said he lay in a hospital bed thinking things like, "This is not real; this can't be real. I am a head, locked in a brace, bolted to the wall. I have no body, no arms, no legs—at least nothing I can sense." Even though Tyler and I had never experienced anything so awful as what Chad shared that night, we were captivated by his message and could relate in a small way to his words. At times, we've both thought, "This is not real, this can't be real" in some of the situations we've found ourselves in.

In his book *Doing What Must Be Done*, Chad shared how he felt boredom, futility, and hopelessness engulf him as he lay "staring at the stark white composite ceiling." He said of that terrible time, "I [could] no longer hope to accomplish the dreams that lent enthusiasm and energy to my life." Though I had very little reason to feel this futile about my own life, I certainly could understand a bit of what Chad felt because I had thought similar things regarding my food addiction. Though our stories were vastly different, I noticed some similarities having to do with the words we were choosing to think about our individual circumstances.

I'm sure you have had similar thoughts at times as well when life has thrown you curveballs you were not expecting. I'm sure you've felt disappointment, pain, and uncertainty about what the next step ought to be on your journey. Maybe you've not been able to sleep some nights, rehearsing all the things you feel you have no control over. Maybe your thoughts have become consumed with such worries as "This is not how I thought life would go. This is not what I wanted. This isn't fair. This can't be real."

But as Chad teaches, discovering how to *accept* life on life's terms is vital to our happiness if we are ever to become all we are meant to be. Once he *acknowledged* his situation and began *asking* how he could best deal with it, Chad was able to *accept* it for what it was. Even though his story is bigger and more consequential than most, we can still learn for ourselves what he ultimately learned: Whatever happens to us, we have the power to decide how we are going to show up in life.

Chad's father helped him get to that place of acceptance. "As thoughts darken my mood, in comes the cavalry to the rescue," Chad writes in his book. "It's Dad." Although his father didn't know what it was like to be paralyzed, he had his own experiences that taught him about *accepting*. Three months before Chad's accident, his dad was attending a national business convention in Dallas. The keynote speaker was Hall of Famer Art Berg, a C6-quadriplegic from Salt Lake City. Chad's dad was captivated by Berg's message and never would have guessed that just three months after hearing Berg speak, his son would be lying in a hospital room, starting his own difficult journey as a quadriplegic.

At the hospital, Chad's dad spoke to him. "Son, what if I told you that you could be happier, more productive, and more successful with no hands and no legs than you ever were with them?" Of course, Chad didn't believe this—his thoughts didn't allow him to—not yet. Then Chad's dad shared the 'Art Berg' signature speech, "The Impossible Just Takes a Little Longer," with him.

"A few weeks later, my hospital room door suddenly bumps open and in rolls Art Berg,"

Chad continues. "He doesn't say his name; he doesn't say 'Hi, Chad.' He doesn't say anything. He just wheels over to my bed, picks himself up out of his chair, and throws himself onto my bed." Chad was amazed by Art's mobility because he didn't know it was possible. His brain began to ask empowering questions: "How does he do that?" This was the beginning of a shift in Chad's perspective when he stopped asking "why" and started asking "how" (remember this principle from Chapter 3). Chad was inspired by Art's visit and realized this: "He is challenging me to challenge my own beliefs."

Like Chad, challenging our beliefs is what I believe we all get to do throughout our lives and how we begin putting on the Power Word *accept*. Once you challenge your beliefs, you are able to move forward by exploring new ideas. You can apply the wisdom of Brené Brown, American professor, author, and researcher on shame, who has said this about accepting life for what it is: "Authenticity is the daily practice of letting go of whom we think we're supposed to be and embracing who we are." To put on acceptance is a daily practice. We must learn to redirect our thoughts toward the good each day despite our life circumstances.

The words you put on the matter as you begin to *accept* your life and challenge your beliefs. I have learned to do this by choosing carefully which words I use to label myself and my circumstances. For instance, rather than thinking something like, "I'm a hopeless food addict," I might think something like, "I am addicted to food right now, but I can take a step forward to start overcoming that addiction. My addiction is *not* hopeless." Challenging your negative thoughts allows you to see a clearer path toward growth and progression. In this way, you can **accept** and have the courage to step forward on that path to create the beautiful life you are meant to live.

Accepting Allows You to "Choose Happy"

Several years back, I had the opportunity to serve in the women's organization of my church. It was a responsibility I never anticipated or felt qualified to do, but I decided to give it my best efforts. As I served, I began to notice that as women, we had more in common than not. No matter how young or old or what her story was, each woman in the organization desired to be happy. Naturally, the human spirit craves happiness and peace. I pondered this idea, and one morning as I sat in my favorite spot having some quiet time, a simple wooden sign I had purchased a few years previous caught my attention. Printed in black letters were the words "Choose Happy." I thought about those words each morning while I pondered about my day, and over time I realized that *choosing* to be happy is the essence of *accepting*.

No matter what is going on in your life, you have a choice, and by *accepting* your life as it is at this moment, you can choose to be happy. I have found myself saying on many occasions, "This is not the plan," regarding big and little things in my life. There really is little in life that you have the ability to choose, but your attitude is something over which you have total control. Michael J. Fox, iconic actor, author, and advocate whom I had a crush on when a little girl was diagnosed at just twenty-nine with Parkinson's Disease, has said, "My happiness grows in direct proportion to my acceptance and in inverse proportion to my expectations." To me, Michael J. Fox had everything going for him as a TV icon, yet even he has had to learn how to "choose happy." Being rich, famous, or living a life a privilege doesn't take away problems. Everyone finds themselves saying, "This is not the plan," at times in their life. It is learning to choose how you want to feel each day despite the circumstances of your life that matter.

As I thought about the ladies in my church whom I served, the idea came to me to make a "Choose Happy" sign for each of them—a simple reminder that whether we are joyful or miserable is entirely up to each of us. Each morning as I started my day and read those words, I was consciously putting them on in my life, and they were making a difference in how I *accepted* and felt peace. Why not share this message with others? With the help of some women, I served with, we were able to deliver one hundred signs to the ladies in my church organization. I'm so thankful that God whispered to my heart that these words had the power to help many make choosing happiness a daily habit.

All of us want to feel joy but often get stuck in a place of darkness by the words we choose to think. Mark Williamson, director of *Action for Happiness*, said, "Our society puts huge pressure on us to be successful and to constantly compare ourselves with others. This causes a great deal of unhappiness and anxiety. If we can learn to be more accepting of ourselves as we really are, we're likely to be much happier. . . Our day-to-day habits have a much bigger impact on our happiness than we might imagine."

These habits include the words we put on and think. Words absolutely *do* have such power, and as you start to accept where you are each day, you "choose happy." Some days you will want to make that choice, and some days you won't, but over time I have found that as I put on the Word Effect's Power Words, they become a part of me. These words are reminders and triggers to keep me moving forward in the direction I desire to go. When my mind starts to take the negative path it has become so accustomed to, the words I put on stop me and direct my attention toward the path of acceptance and peace.

Now, choosing happy doesn't mean you and I won't have times of sadness, discouragement, despondency, and doubt; we can all still wander into a fog sometimes. What it does mean, however, is that we have the power (or words) to help us find happiness despite the circumstances we find ourselves in. As you *accept* your current circumstances, you will focus on the good and search for truth, which will help you move forward out of that fog. The words you think, say to yourself and put on consistently can make such a difference in your life. I have learned the sun will come out again even after struggling through the worst of storms when we choose the right words to put on each day.

To conclude this chapter, I encourage you to take to heart this suggestion from Deborah Reber, writer of *Chicken Soup for the Teenage Soul*: "Letting go," or as I would say, *accepting* what is, "doesn't mean that you don't care about someone anymore. It's just realizing that the only person you really have control over is yourself." Acceptance starts from within. Stop looking at everyone else's life and begin to live your own. Although you may not have the beautiful life you want *yet*, finding joy in your present life is essential to creating your beautiful life.

I encourage you to live a life of "what is" instead of "what if." When you live this way, you find a better balance. Remember, all is as it should be, right at this moment. You are exactly *who* and *where* you should be today. Once you *accept* this truth, you will be ready to move on to all you can become tomorrow. We will begin learning how to do this in the next chapter as we explore Power Word 4 in the Word Effect, which is *abundance*.

Before going on to Chapter 5, however, please take the following challenge. As you do, you will feel the flow of the Word Effect; you will see how you are able to create the life you want despite the things that happen to you. As you continue focusing on the good, taking personal responsibility, and choosing happy, you can then stop perching precariously on that one-legged stool and become more balanced and ready to become all you are intended to be.

Challenge Your Resistance to Change by Accepting What Is Now: Three Self-Acceptance Ideas to "Put On" Daily

1. Remember to *acknowledge* your desires and *ask* questions using "how" instead of "why." Then, practice *accepting* "what is" instead of looking for "what if." Start now by describing your "what is" in positive words: _____

    _____

    _____

    _____

2. Focus on the good. Each day practice looking for the good of the moment instead of the negative. Remember, *acceptance* means allowing things to unfold exactly how they unfold. Each time you notice a negative thought, practice putting on an accepting thought. For example, you might find yourself thinking, "I didn't get all the things done on my to-do list." Notice this thought and then think something true but positive about your situation: "But I did get two of the five things done on my list" or "But I did help my friend who really needed support."

3. Put the words "choose happy" in your life by keeping them somewhere you can see every day. When you notice these words, really stop and absorb them. Decide right then how you can choose to be happy, no matter what is going on at that moment.

"Being happy doesn't mean that everything is perfect. It means that you've decided to look beyond the imperfections."
—Unknown

CHAPTER 5

ABUNDANCE

THE POWER WORD THAT FOCUSES YOUR ATTENTION ON PROGRESS OVER PERFECTION

---

*"Abundance is not something we acquire.
It is something we tune into."*
—Wayne Dyer

Power Word 4: *Abundance – (noun): a large quantity of something.*

Every December here in Utah, I enjoy the freshly fallen snow as we near the Christmas holiday. I don't seem to mind the white blanket that covers everything or the cold temperatures leading up to my much anticipated "white Christmas." On those occasions when the desired snow has not fallen and everything appears brown and dead, I have, in the past, felt quite disappointed and let down. But as much as I might wish to wake up to snow on Christmas morning, this, like so many things in life, is something over which I have absolutely no control.

While a white Christmas is nothing more than a circumstance, a fact, it's what I choose to think about that fact that gives the circumstance any meaning. The set of words I choose to put on regarding the rather inconsequential fact of snow or no snow on Christmas morning is what causes how I feel. And that feeling is not so inconsequential, since how I feel drives the actions I take or don't take, which then creates the outcomes of my life.

When I have felt disappointed about the lack of snow, I have usually thought something like, "It should have snowed for Christmas, and now everything seems dull and drab. I just won't be able to feel the magic of the holiday." But as I've learned to apply the Word Effect in my life, I've discovered that anytime I think the word *should*, it leads me to feel as if I lack for something, which leads to misery. When I am disappointed, the actions I take center around negative emotions.

To go along with our example, at Christmas time I might be less likely to focus on all the amazing blessings in my life as I celebrate the birth of Jesus Christ, participate in family time, and make holiday memories. When I put on a genuine thought like "I am thankful for this holiday season" instead, I feel content, which makes it possible for me to look up and out and focus on the good. When I am content, I can stop being an emotional child and shun the negativity bias that would otherwise take hold. Feelings of lack are replaced with feelings of abundance.

Approaching life with the Power Word *abundance* brings transformative momentum into your life. That's why *abundance* is one of the seven Power Words in the Word Effect cycle of becoming—a word by which I now live and want to share with you throughout this chapter.

> *Choosing to focus on the* **abundance** *in your life will let you become content and open you to the possibility of receiving even more of life's bountiful blessings. It will give you the courage to dream bigger and act on those dreams in a positive way where you can focus on progress rather than perfection in your efforts to create your most beautiful life.*

Throughout the remainder of this chapter, I want to share with you the significance and beauty of putting the word *abundance* on each day. We will explore how to become more content, how to dream bigger, and how to act on the good and let go of the negative. This all begins as you focus on the good, which is available to you in great abundance!

Abundant thinking is a powerful way to keep the momentum going in your life so you can continue the process of becoming your best self.

Being Content with What Is Opens You to Receive More

The Power Word *abundance* goes hand in hand with *accept* (Power Word 3), which we covered in the last chapter. Just as *accepting* where you are right now can bring you quickly to a place of peace and happiness, approaching your life from a place of *abundance* allows you to better focus on the good, no matter where you are at this very moment. With practice, this perspective can bring almost immediate contentment, which prepares you to receive even more abundance in your life.

Living with an abundant mentality means we stop looking for the good things we *don't* have and start seeing the good things we *do* have. And when we focus on the good already present in our lives, we feel happy, and the way naturally opens for us to receive more blessings and goodness. Even if the Christmases of life tend to be more brown, cold, and lackluster than white, sparkling, and pure, life can still be amazing, depending on *how* you approach it—either from a place of discontent or a place of abundance.

My own love-hate relationship with Utah's snowy weather aptly illustrates this principle. While I so badly long for snow all through December, I'm completely over the desire by the time January's blizzards roar in like a lion! Just a week or two after Christmas, I am ready for spring again, but if you know Utah's Rocky Mountain winter, you know that the snow and the cold are just settling in for at least another three months. Those pesky snowflakes fall and fall. If I choose to focus on how I don't like to drive in snowy weather, don't like to be cold, and don't like how gray and dark everything is, then winter can be pretty dreadful. But when I change my mindset and focus on the good of each and every day, I find an abundance of goodness no matter how much it snows, and I discover how to feel peace and contentment amid my circumstances.

What a wonderful word *content* is, especially when you consider how little any of us control in life (such as the weather). Google's English dictionary provides a few different definitions of the word content. One definition of *content* is a state of peaceful happiness. As a prayerful person, I have loved reading the simple meditations found in the book *Twenty-Four Hours a Day.* The prayer passage for June 11 reads simply, "I pray that today I may have inner peace. I pray that today I may be at peace with myself." When I put on words like *abundance, gratitude,* and *peace,* I focus on my blessings. The feeling of contentment settles over me, despite the uncertainty of life, and prepares me for all the good that is still coming.

It might seem difficult to be content, at peace, and satisfied with the life you are living, but it is actually quite easy to feel you are already abundantly blessed. Some snowy days will be beautiful, and others will seem gray and icy. Which day do you find yourself perceiving the most? Presuming that every day and situation should be perfect, pretty, and painless means you will always be discontent, and life will *never* be enough. Moreover, if you never experience the icy and dreadful snow days, you won't be able to enjoy the fresh, crisp snow days—or the sunny days of spring that come later. For everything, there is an opposite; it's how you *perceive* that opposite that determines how much you learn, grow, and find meaning and joy.

When you put on the Power Word *abundance* every day, you choose to have an entirely grateful approach to everything in life, including the brown and cold, the dark and dreary. I love the words of the religious hymn "Count Your Many Blessings" by Johnson Oatman. The lyrics encourage you to "count your blessings; name them one by one. Count your blessings; see what God hath done." When was the last time you counted the good things in your life instead of focusing on the bad? To come to life from a place of *abundance* is to count the blessings before you. It is to look beyond what isn't going right so you can fix your gaze on positivity, which prepares your heart to receive even more positivity.

You can find power in music such as "Count Your Many Blessings" but also in the words you think, read, hear, and speak. Remember how much my life changed when I became more aware of the power of words? Now, I am very aware of the words I think, speak, hear, and read; if they don't make me feel good, I have the power to change that! I can choose better words—Power Words such as *abundance*. Keeping my thoughts, heart, and mind in an *abundant* mentality—in a state of constant gratitude and contentment—is a part of my life-long journey to create the most beautiful life I can possibly imagine.

Also, remember from our discussions in previous chapters that your belief system (which is based on the set of repetitive words you use to describe your feelings) drives your behavior and, thus, the outcomes you experience. What you think about, you bring about. The health, wealth, happiness, and success you enjoy rest squarely on the quality of your internal dialogue. I think this idea bears repeating:

The health, wealth, happiness, and success you have rest squarely on the quality of your internal dialogue.

Consider these self-talk examples that indicate a negative belief system steeped in an attitude of permanent and pervasive discontent and scarcity rather than contented abundance—do any of them sound familiar?

- I never have enough time to get everything done. There's no way we will make our deadlines this month so we can invoice clients and get paid.
- Why can't my kid just pick up after herself? She's draining all the energy out of me.
- I never get the promotion; it always goes to someone else. I'm so sick of being passed over.
- I always feel so down when I wake up. Am I ever going to feel happy again about anything?
- Why is it so impossible for me to eat healthily for longer than a day or two? What's wrong with me?
- The laundry never seems to get completely done . . . I would, for once, just like to sit in a clean, completely organized house.
- How come my friend doesn't call me back whenever I reach out to her? I never feel like I have a friend in her.
- Why doesn't my spouse bring home flowers anymore? He used to be so attentive . . . Now I feel like we have no more romance in our relationship.

Now consider what happens to your perception of the world when the words you use to think about your circumstances come from a place of *abundance*:

- I'm so thankful we have all this work! I might have to hire someone to help me get it done so we can invoice on time.
- My daughter has made so much progress in getting her dirty clothes in the hamper; she doesn't throw everything on the floor anymore.
- I'm going to ask for a raise since I haven't been promoted yet. I've been doing a lot of extra work, and I want to be paid for it.
- I want to get more sleep. I'm going to bed on time this week so I can wake up feeling better.
- I need to get help with my food addictions; I can't possibly handle this anymore by myself.
- Time for a new chore chart . . . My kids will benefit if they learn responsibility and do all their own laundry each week.
- I don't have time to worry about why my friend hasn't called me back. I have friends and neighbors who are lonely or need my support! I'm glad I have time to give them.
- My spouse goes to work at 3 a.m. every day and works so hard for our family. I'm so thankful for all he does, and I want to show him how much I appreciate him.

These positive words can completely shift your perspective from a feeling of bitterness to a powerful mentality of abundance and gratitude. When you look at things from an *abundant* viewpoint, you take control back and have the power to become content and happy. If you practice enough, you can shift your attitude *instantly by choosing to focus on the good*. Isn't that amazing? And what's more, these thoughts will often put you in a position to attract even more blessings into your life. It's as if an abundance of blessings is predicated on your first being satisfied with the tiniest amount of good fortune.

I know this to be true because I have seen God work this way in my life. I know He wants nothing more than to shower me with hope, peace, joy, and beauty. But He must follow the laws of nature, which dictate that I cannot receive more until I am content and satisfied with what I already have, no matter how small that is. Once I see that goodness and feel a sense of *abundance* about it—even if it doesn't seem like much—then the Almighty can pour out blessings upon me in so much abundance that "there shall not be room enough to receive" them, as it states in Malachi 3:10 of the Old Testament. I know this can be the case for you as well.

One of the easiest ways to understand this principle is by living the Law of Tithing, which is taught by God in many passages of scripture (including the Old and New Testaments of the Bible, the Torah, and others). While this law may seem to be some kind of religious practice having to do with the way money is collected in a church to help fund it, I am here to tell you that it is so much more than that. This is a law that teaches *abundant* thinking and living. It is a law God has given us to help us be generous in our approach to ourselves, others, and life in general—to help us learn not to be greedy, stingy, and anxious but rather to loosen our grip and attract an abundance of goodness into our lives.

I find it interesting that some of the world's most successful financial gurus are living the Law of Tithing, giving money to a church, charity, or to those in need because they know giving to others causes money to naturally flow back to them. They have made this practice a part of their strategic plans for financial success.

Now I'm not suggesting you should pay tithing to your church or give to a charity just so you can attract more money to yourself. My point in mentioning tithing is that it teaches perfectly the idea that when you are generous with what you have, even if it is only a little (think of the widow's mite as found in Luke 21:1–4 of the Bible), you curb dissatisfied and discontent feelings. Giving to others of not only your money but also your time, talents, positive energy, and love opens you up to all that is meant to be yours. Being satisfied with what you have and even being willing to share it can calm your fears and lead you to your beautiful life.

Dare to Dream Bigger

I mentioned numerous times in the last section that as your sense of *abundance* brings you more contentment, you become ready to welcome some truly amazing blessings into your life. You might be wondering how those great blessings really come about. Well, I'm here to tell you that they come because *abundance* places you in a state of mind where you dare to dream bigger.

You'll remember that I started a positive T-shirt and apparel business, Becoming Threads, with my sister-in-law Erin. When it turned two years old, we decided to throw a party. It wasn't just any party but one, of course, that had to do with the power found in words. Our theme was "Dream Bigger," and we centered the event around creating "dream boards," our version of a vision board.

We invited our guests to join us for an evening of inspiration, goodness, and upliftment and to think about the possibility of dreaming bigger. Part of the night's events would be to put ideas and words on paper that inspired each person to continue to pursue their current visionary projects but also to express even bigger dreams—some of the most significant desires of their heart.

As we began to invite people, many on our guest list sounded excited and would say things like, "I would love to do this! I have always wanted to design a vision board and become more intentional with my dreams, but I've never taken the time." This was a common sentiment we heard as we prepared for the fun gathering. But as I reached out to one friend we had invited to see if she was coming, she looked at me and said matter-of-factly, "No." The "no" wasn't the hard part to hear—it was the words she shared after that left a lasting impression on me: "I'm not coming because I have decided to stop dreaming. I no longer dream because none of my goals or pursuits, or desires ever happen. If I don't dream, then I don't have to fail. I always fail or don't achieve my desires, so why dream?"

As I thought about her utterly demoralizing and deflating thought processes, I knew her beliefs about never accomplishing anything had nothing to do with who she was as a person. She was incredibly capable and in fact had achieved and been blessed with many wonderful things in her life. The truth behind why she wasn't realizing any of her dreams had to do with the thoughts she was putting on about who she was as a person. She was focusing on her own perceived deficiencies. Her scarcity mentality kept her stuck in a place of negative discontent. She saw no *abundance* in her life because she used a negative set of words to define her thoughts and therefore lacked the courage to aspire to anything bigger. She had decided that she was unable to accomplish her dreams, and she continued to prove that to herself every day. Remember, what you think about, you bring about. Everything starts with your thoughts.

The fact is, the other guests we had invited, who were cheerfully and excitedly looking forward to the event, were also, at times, unable to realize their dreams. But they were choosing not to focus on that fact alone; the words they used to think about their life were grounded in the abundance of good they saw and hoped to bring into their life. They were open to focusing on their future self with possibility and wonder instead of their past self, full of fear and dread. In their RSVPs, a sense of hope, anticipation, and growth seemed to jump out at us. The reason my friend had decided to stop dreaming was that the thought "My dreams never come true" doesn't generate feelings of contentment, determination, or courageous intention. The words she chose to put on were discouraging, and thus she felt discouraged. Her actions reflected this, causing her to stop dreaming.

Despite trying to convince her to attend, in the end, my friend didn't show up. She failed ahead of time, missing the opportunity to put out into the universe the deepest desires of her heart. She continued to look for evidence from her past of all the ways she would fall short. The result she created was an attitude of fear. She stopped having the courage to dream, to approach life as if it would deliver abundantly, and instead entrenched herself further into a world of scarcity.

If you're wondering whether you have the courage to dream bigger, ask yourself what words you are thinking today. I hope, after reading this far, that you are now more aware of your words and thoughts. Words are free to all of us; the power found in them is universal, and that's why the Word Effect is so influential in our process of becoming. Our words form our thoughts, and our thoughts drive everything, including our ability to achieve our dreams.

Any time you start trying to realize your dreams—especially those dreams you have never done before—you'll almost always feel a lot of excitement and anticipation of joy, at least initially. Once you begin the process, however, you may learn about many difficult things you have to do to fulfill your dreams. In my case, I had never attempted to write a book before this one. The spark that led me to take the first step dimmed as my focus easily shifted to what I lacked instead of what abilities and resources I had to assist me. I had this same experience when I launched Becoming Threads, built a coaching and mentoring group, worked to become a public speaker, and especially as I intentionally tried to be a good wife and mother.

One thought that held me captive for a long time as I wrote this book was, "I should have finished the book by now." Though this sounds innocent, it is not. The thought didn't make me feel content. It created feelings of overwhelm and scarcity. When I would sit down to write, the idea that I wasn't making progress took all the joy out of the process, and instead of the words flowing abundantly and freely, my creativity shut down. The result I created for myself was a continued delay in finishing the book, which only served to prove to myself (and to others, I mistakenly thought) that I was unable to accomplish important things in my life.

But when I stopped to ask myself what words I was using to think about the project, I realized they were negative and from a scarcity mindset. I had lost sight of the reason for writing in the first place as well as how much I'd already written. As I focused more on approaching the writing from an abundant mindset, the words came more easily. It's certainly been a long and not-always-easy journey, but focusing on gratitude and abundance along the way has made a huge difference in my ability to chase my dreams.

Progress, Not Perfection

In previous chapters, I have shared with you how from an early age I was plagued by perfectionism and how I expected perfection not only in myself but in others. When I assumed I could not be content or happy until everything was done just right, I was certainly not in a mindset of *abundance*. Some faulty thinking I picked up early on in life was that being perfect meant being free of error. But ironically, in order to become more perfect, we must embrace the fact that there will be some failure in what we pursue and view it as a wonderful part of our progression.

In fact, I like to call *failure* a "growth opportunity" (because, let's face it, *failure* is such a harsh word). In the experiment of life, we must try things, gather information, and learn what works and what doesn't. This process of failing and learning doesn't mean we are worthless. None of us are forever failures, even though we will experience plenty of imperfections in life. Accepting that life is a quest (or growth opportunity) with unknown outcomes can help us ditch the perfectionism mentality and focus on making progress instead. And the key to experiencing that mindset shift is *abundance*.

Life tests that result in supposed "failures" can often feel very uncomfortable (because the results seem flawed), but this discomfort is actually a sign that we are growing and making progress. The Word Effect has helped me understand this—that I don't have to be perfect (and neither does anyone else) and that progress rather than perfection is the desired way to live. No one is perfect, so when we pressure ourselves with perfectionism, we kill all abundant thought. Let me repeat this:

When we pressure ourselves with perfectionism,
we kill all abundant thought.

Since abundant thought is what allows us to make progress and not get stuck in the negative, unreachable, impossible place of perfectionism, we must learn how to put this Power Word on more and more intentionally.

Think about the word *perfectionism*. When we seek to be perfect and for everyone else to be as well, we are automatically implying that we or another person are not good enough. It assumes failure as opposed to accomplishment. Rather than spurring us on to greater achievement and becoming the best version of ourselves, perfectionism serves to confound and immobilize us. If making progress and becoming better is your goal, perfectionism is no way to get there. This mentality has words associated with it, such as pettiness, quibbling, fault-finding, hair-splitting, and criticism. We all know that these bring stagnation rather than progress.

When we focus on the "not enough" in ourselves, we then begin to see not enough in others, too. In Richard Paul Evan's book *The Four Doors*, he explains the concept of the "crab mentality," a phrase that refers to the dynamic of a pot full of crabs. "Individually, the crabs could easily climb out of the pot," explains Evans, "except that the other crabs will pull down any crab that tries to escape. The analogy to the human condition is obvious. It is a common social phenomenon that members of a group will attempt to 'pull down' any individual member who achieves success beyond the others. The mindset is, 'If I can't have it, neither can you.' Instead of being inspired by others' success, small-minded people resent others' achievements because of fear that they are being left behind."

Demanding unachievable perfection of ourselves often leads to seeking perfection in others. This "crab mentality," where we assume everyone else is just as flawed as we perceive ourselves to be, propels us to find fault, criticize, nit-pick, and so forth. Like the crabs in the pot, we drag others down and ourselves right along with them. Our focus will become our reality. If we think nobody is good enough, those thoughts will always prove true—at least in our own minds. This is flawed thinking!

Instead, when you feel the need to perfect, criticize, or be annoyed, I urge you to stop and apply the Power Word *abundance* to your thinking. You have goodness in your life already, no matter how little. You have the power to improve and progress. *Abundance* allows you to move along at the pace that's right for you, and it permits others to move forward along their own path in the timing that is right before them and God. The power of just one word can change everything!

Acting on the Abundance of Goodness in Your Life

Most human beings have one thing in common: the desire for a good life. And when we enjoy an abundance of goodness, we often desire to share that goodness with others. We should not only share our own abundance but also learn to be willing to receive the bounty others have to share. When we give and receive, all are blessed, as the scripture found in 2 Corinthians 8:14 of the Bible confirms: "But by an equality, that now at this time your abundance may be a supply for their want, that their abundance also may be a supply for your want:

that there may be equality." As each one of us acts on our desires to help others, equality, fairness, and—most importantly—peace abound.

Several years ago, while becoming awakened by the power of words, I decided to set and act on two goals (dreams) having to do with instilling this power more fully in my life. The first goal I set was to join the church choir. I have always wanted to be a singer but had put on the thought that I really have little talent for it, and that thought had then become a belief. However, I still had a desire to become better at singing and decided to pursue this dream with courage, feeling like I had something to offer. The great thing about the church choir is you don't have to audition, and they won't kick you out! So, I began attending practices and learned as I went along.

I realized there were many people who knew how to read music and the vocal parts much better than myself; I had only a small idea of how to do it. But as I asked questions, and, most importantly, showed up to as many practices as possible, I began to improve. My actions, taken from a place of abundance and not scarcity, allowed me to develop talents I did not think I had. But something even more remarkable started to happen. I began to pay closer attention to the words we were singing. The music and words began to penetrate my heart and soul. Many songs we practiced and sang were ones I had grown up singing while going to church each week but singing them this time around was different. The words were telling a story, and the story included me in it every single time.

As the words began to have more and more meaning in my life, I found myself on several occasions thinking about a phrase or set of words from a song we had been practicing that would help me throughout my week. These powerful words put to music helped me see just how richly and abundantly blessed my life was, which led me to have a grander view of all the good that was within my reach to both receive and give.

Attending practices and learning words that would fill my soul as I sang them was much like taking a hot air balloon ride that lifted me up above the pollution and smog of city life. As I rose up in the air in a slow and steady climb, only a few things were visible at first. But eventually, everything gave way to revealing an expansive view, allowing me to see things differently from a more complete perspective. While I can't change the smog, I can rise above it. There, I can see the abundance of good in my life and choose to share it with others. Singing in the choir, despite my lack of developed talent, was just one way I chose to share my abundance. Giving what I could blessed me, but I feel it also blessed others. I continue to sing in my church choir today, sharing my small talents with others and receiving from those in the choir who are more abundantly blessed with musical skills. As I do, feelings of *abundance* continue to grow within me.

I set my second goal after attending a leadership meeting for a youth organization I served in. One of the other leaders asked us if we realized whom some of the girls in the group were following on Instagram. She told us that since you can look at which members of Instagram follow whom, out of curiosity and concern, she had checked out the "following" lists of the girls' Instagram accounts. She was dismayed by some of the unwholesome influences the young women were willingly bringing into their lives.   After the meeting, I had a strong prompting that I was capable of posting uplifting and inspiring words to the world. I decided to do this in the form of a positive quote on my social media page every day for an entire year using the hashtag "#sharegoodness." I knew that several of the girls were following me and decided to try to influence them with an abundance of goodness in the hopes it would sort of "cancel out" the negativity, smut, and filth otherwise filling their minds on social media.

Deciding which quote to use on any given day was easy—I simply used whatever words had significance for me on that day. So, if I was feeling impatient, I would search for quotes on patience and choose the one that resonated with me. If I was feeling ungrateful, I would post about gratitude. The amazing thing I discovered in the process was that although these words were meant to help the girls, they played a major role in my own mental well-being and desire for goodness.

Again, the Word Effect influenced my own life in a powerful way as I acted on promptings to help others by sharing my *abundance*. Acting on goodness always has a reciprocal effect: Following through on this prompting not only had the potential to help those girls but also gave me a greater desire to be more open to the beauty within me. Because I shared my abundance, my abundance grew, and I developed my writing and speaking talents and launched a coaching career to keep sharing it.

As I began to change my focus, my reality began to change. When I looked for the good, I began to be more and more plentifully blessed with it. Seeing goodness abound in my life and sharing it with others allowed me to knock down the wall of scarcity I had built around my soul. I realized from this experience that there is plenty of goodness and love in the world, but it is often through words that we can focus on that good and figure out how to best use our time, energy, and abilities to spread it to others.

As I began to change my words, other promptings came into my life with ways to share their power with others. One of those ways came to me as I searched for T-shirts with positive messages on them before I started my company. Remember that moment when I pulled a shirt off the rack and the heavens seemed to open? "Why don't you start putting positive messaging on T-shirts yourself? If you are looking for this type of apparel, there's probably someone else looking for it also. There might be a need out there for this. Why don't you share goodness with others?"

As soon as the thought of imprinting empowering messages entered my mind, my heart felt a surge of *abundance* as if it were being filled from above. But as quickly as this inspired idea came, the negative self-talk followed. "T-shirts? That isn't exactly an original and unique concept, Becky. There are T-shirts everywhere . . . How is this a good idea?" Immediately my brain put the brakes on. A scarcity mentality took over, which tends to paralyze me. I felt the prompting but began to analyze it instead of just acting on it.

Stephen Covey has said this about the scarcity mentality:

> "Most people are deeply scripted in what I call the Scarcity Mentality. They see life as having only so much, as though there were only one pie out there. And if someone were to get a big piece of the pie, it would mean less for everybody else."

My brain was following that script, thinking that with so many successful T-shirt companies out there, the world simply didn't have room for another one. This scarcity mentality I immediately adopted at the thought of creating my inspired shirts came from my cerebellum, or my lower brain, which I have also heard called the primitive or lizard brain. This primitive brain is motivated by three things: conserving energy, avoiding pain, and seeking pleasure. If we don't manage our lower brain, we will never live in a place of abundance where the higher brain functions in the prefrontal cortex take place.

While the primitive brain's job is to keep you safe and stuck in a cave, the prefrontal cortex or the higher brain's job is to help you progress out of the stone age. Every time you decide to step out of your cave to experience something new, the primitive brain will scream at you to get safely back inside. What's so wonderful about the Word Effect is that words have the power to yank you out of the primitive thinking of the lower brain. The right set of words can help you form the right thoughts, which can then take you out of the lizard brain's reactionary, survivalist thinking and into the middle region of the brain, or the limbic system, where feelings are processed.

Those feelings then affect the way the higher brain, the prefrontal cortex, reasons and processes information so you can make calculated decisions about the way you will act. This chain reaction puts the control of your behavior back in your hands and out of the lizard brain, helping you have the courage to step out and take action. When I had the thought that imprinted T-shirts were nothing new, I didn't know that my lower brain was motivating me to conserve energy and avoid pain by objecting to the impression to start something potentially risky. I was focused on my past self and didn't have enough evidence to prove to my higher brain that I could succeed. With my focus there, my brain continued to point out all the ways in which I was lacking and kept me stuck in my cave.

As I argued back and forth with my lower brain, a clear and simple thought came: "T-shirts are always needed, and this type is different. These aren't just any T-shirts, Becky; their purpose is to influence and uplift the wearer. Sharing powerful words through these tees will not only help you *become*—other women who put them on will be changed by the words they choose to wear each day."

Thank goodness I listened to the still and small voice that nudged me in the direction to start Becoming Threads. Deciding to show up and use my prefrontal cortex to launch this venture (with the help of my business partner, Erin) has opened me up to so much *abundance*. Everything that happened in the days and weeks leading up to my having this idea came about so I could learn and grow.

In addition to the obvious monetary benefits I enjoyed from running a small business, I also received more joy, contentment, and peace than I did before taking on this project because I was sharing goodness all around; I was abundantly blessed for my efforts. This experience taught me that we can either embrace or miss out on the abundance of goodness in the world.

Having an abundance of goodness, joy, peace, and hope doesn't just come flying to us on the wings of wishful thinking. *Abundance* means working and making an effort *consistently* over time. When the stingy, scarce, "not enough" feelings settle in—and they will come—we will need to stop and ask ourselves what words we are using to think about our circumstances. The thoughts are what we want to challenge, not our feelings.

Catching your negative, scarcity-focused words and thoughts early is the key. Those negative thoughts will come because you have unintentionally conditioned your mind to focus there; you have allowed your lizard brain to control you. But you have the power to feel differently, and that power comes from consciously putting on abundant words each day.

When I find myself slipping back into my old worrisome thoughts, I remind myself that they didn't serve me well. Then I make the choice to refuse to entertain them. I toss them off instead, like a shirt I decided doesn't look good on me today. Then I begin to look for the good. I invite you to do the same. Learn to lift your focus on your abundance so your perspective will show you the blessings in your life instead of what isn't going as planned. As you focus on your good, it then becomes so much easier to give that goodness away to someone else. Your life can become richer, more full, and more abundant, and this is what allows you to dream bigger, make progress, and share your goodness with others.

Of course, there will always be hills to climb and mountains to scale, but climbing above the negativity affords a pretty spectacular view. I have seen it, and that is what keeps me coming back for more. I urge you to keep coming back despite the events that happen on life's terms. When you look up and look out at your life circumstances, be grateful that you are in the process of becoming the best version of yourself.

To conclude this chapter, I encourage you to take a closer look at your own life to see where you feel you are either lacking or have been abundantly blessed. Before going on to Chapter 6, be sure to complete the following challenge that can help you identify where you might want to practice putting more gratitude in your life. As Tony Robbins has said, "When you are grateful, fear disappears, and abundance appears." This feeling of abundance will help you feel more content, have greater courage to act on your dreams, make true progress, and give you the desire to share the goodness of your life with others. When you have completed the challenge, join me as we step forward to the next chapter, where we will explore the Power Word *action*.

Challenge Your Discontent with an Abundance of Gratitude

1. Count your blessings and let's "name them one by one." Take some time to focus on the abundance of good in each of the following areas of your life:

Spiritual: _____

_____

Physical: _____

_____

Mental: _____

_____

Emotional: _____

_____

Social/Interpersonal: _____

_____

2. Did any of those areas feel lacking in abundance? If so, you might try asking these questions: "Am I having fun?" "What do I have to lose?" Both questions are useful when you want to shift your focus to the good. Write your answers and insights here. _____

_____

_____

"The fastest way to bring more wonderful examples of abundance into your personal experience is to take constant notice of the wonderful things that are already there."
—Esther Hicks

CHAPTER 6

ACTION

THE ENERGY AND POWER THAT KEEPS YOU MOVING ALONG THE PATH OF JOYFUL LIVING

"Take the first step in faith. You don't have to see the whole staircase, just take the first step."
—Martin Luther King, Jr.

Power Word 5: *Action (noun) – the fact or process of doing something, typically to achieve an aim.*

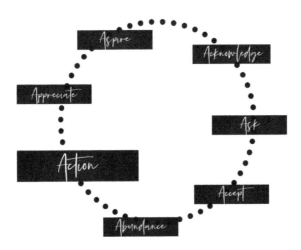

At the end of every summer, our family spends a wonderful week at Lake Powell near the Arizona-Utah border. It is a time we all eagerly look forward to—a chance to get away from the busyness of life, relax, and renew our spirits as well as our relationships with each other. I always pack a few books to read on the trip and a notebook to jot down ideas for the next project I have in mind. I enjoy this down-time that allows me to dream about possibilities and discover more creativity by just being in the present moment.

On one of these trips, I committed to taking some action I had been putting off by noting in my calendar that the first Monday back from our trip, I would clean out the computer closet in my office and spend at least twenty-five minutes writing each day so I could finish up this book. When I was sitting on top of the houseboat looking at my calendar, these small commitments seemed doable and easy. But on Sunday evening right after we got home, I looked at my calendar again to plan for the coming week and saw that I had already set some other goals to work on and couldn't imagine why I thought the closet-cleaning and writing commitment were good ideas! Because I didn't feel like doing those two things and felt the stress of returning home from our trip, it became really easy for me to make excuses for not keeping my commitments that week.

I told myself, "Trying to do these things on Monday right after we get back from vacation was a terrible idea." I began thinking words that stagnated my momentum: "Maybe I will just push these tasks out to another day of the week instead of trying to do them tomorrow. After all, on Monday, I'll need to do the laundry, tidy the house, wash my hair, get my nails done . . ." The list seemed to go on and on. I figured my brain must not have been firing on all cylinders on that houseboat if it had made such silly commitments. "I think I'll just run to Costco instead. Wouldn't that be a better use of my time than sitting down to write or opening the closet?"

As those procrastinating thoughts swirled around in my head, I began to feel overwhelmed, and as we have been learning throughout this book, thoughts and feelings drive our actions. When I was feeling peaceful and serene on the houseboat at Lake Powell, the thoughts I had were empowering; I felt capable of doing these two simple projects, and I had a strong desire and a feeling of certainty that I could get them done. But once I was home and the stress of getting back into regular life loomed over me, I didn't know how I was going to honor my commitments to myself. I was letting the fear of the un known get the best of me. This fear made me put off organizing my house and writing this book over and over again.

Unsure of what to do next, the downward spiral of negativity kept me from taking action that would help me accomplish my true desires. But along with those thoughts came the realization that if I waited to write a chapter and clean out the computer closet until I felt more like doing those things or until the "time was right," I would never get them done.

What I have learned from setting goals and then not being able to get off the ground with them is that a journey we strike out on isn't always the hard part, but taking the first step often is! When you take that first step, you are demonstrating to yourself, God, and others that you want to go forward, you want to change, and you want to make something happen. But in reality, you might not necessarily want to do the work that will be required in each step of your journey. Taking action can be hard!

When I have found myself spiraling down the path of procrastination and coming up with all kinds of excuses for not doing what I need and want to get done, I begin to feel like a failure. I fear that I am inadequate. I stop operating from a place of *abundance* (Power Word 4; see Chapter 5). Instead of taking action, I start focusing on negative thoughts that drive paralyzing, negative emotions. Courage and confidence go out the door.

But when I choose to think things such as "I have been overwhelmed by hard things before and I have managed to accomplish them. I can do this, too" or "Let's just take things one step at a time," I am able to redirect myself up and out of a downward spiral. Sometimes I realize that I am merely perceiving a situation as too hard, too unpleasant, or just plain not what I want to do that day! When I choose to think empowering words, feelings of fear and inadequacy are replaced with feelings of power, motivation, and enthusiasm. Those feelings lead me to *action*, which is one of the seven Power Words in the Word Effect cycle of becoming, and one that I want to help you see can have an amazing effect on your life.

> *By committing to take **action** through small, consistent steps, you will naturally be propelled forward and receive the power needed to continue your journey of self-discovery, personal development, and joyful living. **Action** creates momentum, making it possible to live every day with purpose and accomplishment.*

Throughout the remainder of this chapter, I will show you through the power of the Word Effect how to commit to taking action; how to break that action down into small, digestible steps; and the importance of being consistent in the way you take action. You can be given the strength to continue moving along the path of self-discovery and self-mastery when you apply this important Power Word.

When you first *acknowledge* (Power Word 1) where you are and what you want, you naturally begin to *ask* (Power Word 2) questions—you stay curious. As you *accept* (Power Word 3) where you are right now, without getting down on yourself for being fearful or unsure, and you approach things with a grateful, *abundant* (Power Word 4) heart, you can take steps forward to *act* (Power Word 5) on the answers to your questions. As you move forward, the steps you need to take and the way you need to travel will become clearer.

You already have the power within you to choose words that can create feelings that fuel the right action you need to take to get your desired results. We will discuss the importance of committing fully, taking small steps, and how being consistent will help you show up for yourself daily and ultimately help you create the kind of life you were always meant to live.

Commit Fully to Get into the Game

The principle of the Power Word *action* can be found in the Bible. We see it show up in places like James 1:22:

"But be ye doers of the word, and not hearers only, deceiving your own selves."

How can you be a doer (action taker) and not just someone who stands around watching others take action? I have learned a lot about taking action and not idly sitting by as I have watched the many baseball games my boys have played over the years. It is very easy for me to lounge in my comfy stadium chair on the bleachers and criticize when someone strikes out. *Why didn't they swing at the pitch?* I think. *It looked good to me.*

What I've learned over time about taking action, however, is that without actually getting into the game, it's pretty hard to have the courage or insight to know how to proceed. There will be no way, for instance, to judge what to do when an eighty- to ninety-mile-per-hour fastball is coming at you unless you're the batter standing at home plate. I have come to realize it is much easier to be critical of others not taking the "right" action than to look at myself taking no action at all! If I'm not invested in and committed to the game, I will not see, for example, that the pitcher for the other team is throwing his best pitch to fool the batter.

While standing on home plate watching a fastball coming at me, I may not know whether to hit or wait . . . But if I never swing, I will never get a hit. In the heat of the moment, taking action can be one of the hardest things to do—to swing the bat, to take the step, to commit. But as the famous Babe Ruth has said, "Never let the fear of striking out keep you from playing the game." You must take *action* to create the results you desire. Those actions come from how you feel, and those feelings are generated by your thoughts, and your thoughts are a product of the words you choose to put on every day! It's that simple.

Writing this book has proven to me the importance of taking action if I want to continue moving forward while staying out of the cycle of negativity. The ideas for what to include in the book came easily, but getting those thoughts out of my mind and down on paper felt more challenging. Thoughts about how I had never written a book before kept me from committing to get fully into the game at first, making me feel very inadequate. My brain showed me all the reasons I was falling short, and I proved to myself that what I feared I couldn't do, I couldn't do—at least for a time.

To commit myself to the book-writing game, I had to take small steps of consistent effort to accomplish the goal of getting these Power Words out of my head and onto paper. Stephen Covey said,

"The only limit to your impact is your imagination and commitment."

Once I discovered the power found in the words I put on every day, I was finally able to make and keep commitments (especially to myself) to write about the power of those words. I stopped having an aversion to the work of writing and immersed myself in the imagination and creation needed to complete this project.

Now think of your own goals and desires—things you want to accomplish. How committed are you to getting them done? How much of the game are you willing to play and how much are you willing to do? As we go further into this chapter, I hope you will see that committing yourself fully to the task at hand rather than sitting back and watching the game is the way to really get things rolling.

Taking Action One Small Step at a Time

Once you have committed to making things happen, where do you need to begin to take that action? Usually, not with talking about what you need to do. Talk is cheap, and nothing gets done standing around commiserating about how hard it can be to make an effort. The power of the Word Effect is in its ability to help you consciously use a set of positive words that will allow you to develop helpful feelings about the situations you face, which will, in turn, help you take actions that create the results you truly desire.

I have found the best way to get past procrastinating thoughts and feelings is to break the action I need to take into small, doable steps. So, I've also broken down the process of taking *action* into small, do-able steps. These steps are to assess, confide, anticipate, and plan.

Step 1: Assess Your Words and Thoughts

The first step to help you take *action* is to assess the words and thoughts you are thinking about the action you need to take. Are they positive or negative? Become aware of the words and negativity bias you may have toward your desired action. A good place to start uncovering what you are really thinking and feeling is to do what many people call a "thought download," or write down everything on your mind so you can think clearly. I try to do this every day. I find it best if I write my thoughts down on paper and get them out of my head. This allows me to look at them and separate circumstances from my own opinions or beliefs.

Here are a few good statements to get you started so you can assess what you are really thinking and the words you are using to formulate those thoughts (see the challenge at the end of this chapter to do this exercise in more depth):

- I don't like . . .
- I don't want . . .
- That won't work because . . .
- I've never done it, so . . .
- It's his/her fault because . . .

Let's take the first statement on this list and use me as an example of how to assess your words and thoughts: "I don't like Mondays because I have so much to do after the weekend and I don't know where to start. I am feeling overwhelmed with my to-do list and wish I could get better organized."

Now let's analyze my thought download. In the first sentence, it is a fact that it is Monday (a circumstance we can all agree on), and the weekend is now over (which is another fact or circumstance). The rest of the statement is just words that describe my thoughts. They sound factual, but in reality, they are nothing more than my opinions regarding Mondays. The thought, "I have so much to do after the weekend," is just a thought because someone else could look at my list of things to do and think it is no big deal. Having too much to do isn't a circumstance; it is simply my thought regarding the fact that I have things to do on Monday. The thought makes me feel overwhelmed because of the way I framed it, and from there, I take action (or not) depending on my feelings of being overwhelmed.

One of the actions is wishing I was better organized. And if I'm not careful, that is how I will spend my time . . . wishing I was doing things instead of actually getting them done! The result I am creating for myself is that I am too overwhelmed to get anything done and spend my time thinking about how I should get things done. This result doesn't come because it's Monday; it comes because of the thoughts I am thinking about Monday.

Now it's your turn to do your own "thought download!" Take a few of the previous statements and finish them by writing out the thoughts you have on the prompts above. Once you have written some of these thoughts out, you can then go back and separate what is true (a circumstance) from what is just your thought (a belief). Sifting fact from opinion is how you can become more aware of your words and thoughts so you can decide if they are serving you.

This exercise is very eye-opening and is how I discovered which words I spent my time thinking about over and over. I then had to decide if I really wanted to be thinking those words or having those beliefs, because, ultimately, they affected how well I could take action or not. This practice of doing a "thought download" every day doesn't take a long time—just a few minutes to invest in me—but it has changed my life. I know it can change yours, too. It will help you see how powerful words are! The words you think really do *matter*, and gaining this awareness will change everything if you choose to look at yourself and the thoughts you put on.

Once you are more aware of your words and thoughts, you can choose to change them, especially if they have a negative bias or are not serving you very well. To help you change your words, you can think of a new set of phrases or statements like in these examples:

- "I have done this before, and I can do it again."
- "I can get help from people who know more about this than I do."
- "I have done similar things, and those turned out all right."

- "I never give up. I'm always trying. Even if I get this wrong at first, I can work to correct it."

Step 2: Confide in Someone You Trust

Once you are using a positive set of words about your goals and desires, you are ready to formally commit to the action by saying it out loud to someone. Each time I have decided to do something I wasn't exactly sure how to do (such as starting my T-shirt apparel business, writing this book, or becoming a public speaker), I would share that secret desire of my heart, usually with my husband, Kris—he is always super supportive. Sharing your goals with someone else helps solidify your plans and makes things more real—after all, that plan is not just in your own head anymore. By expressing your thoughts out loud to someone else, you are, in effect, committing to the universe to begin taking action.

However, even if you are sharing your desires with someone supportive like my husband truly is, sharing can be really hard. That's because doing so requires vulnerability. Letting someone in on your intimate secrets, even someone as close to you as a spouse can be intimidating and scary. What if they think your ideas are stupid? What if they shoot them down? What if you're totally off base and don't know it until someone brings you back to reality?

But as Brené Brown has said, "Vulnerability is not winning or losing. It's having the courage to show up when you can't control the outcome." So, even though I have felt unsure at times about exposing my thoughts and desires, even to my husband, talking about them is a way to take a giant leap forward by making myself accountable. Confiding in someone else about your plans can help you break away from your paralysis and take action, even when you may be filled with fear.

Step 3: Anticipate That the "How" Will Be Revealed in the Doing

So, what happens after we commit to the game, replace negatively biased words and thoughts with positive ones, and then risk ourselves by sharing our ideas with others? In my experience, the lizard brain—which will always try to protect us—takes over, attempting to talk us out of moving forward.

For example, after talking with Kris about the T-shirt business, my brain immediately began to think of all the reasons why I wasn't qualified to start up a new company. I would need to take graphic design classes, I reasoned, and business and accounting courses first. But something Kris said yanked me out of that "don't take risks" primitive thinking: "Just take your idea and act on it," he said, assuring me that how to do these things would be revealed as I made a move. He explained how important it was going to be for me to find people who were good at the things I wasn't and ask them to help me do them. He continued to share from his own experiences how I didn't need to know everything to get started: "If you wait to know how to do everything first, you will always be waiting."

As we commit to taking action, keeping it simple, and taking the next step—even when we don't know how to do something—blessings will follow. Most importantly, we'll be blessed to discover the best way to take additional steps. If we refuse to take a step until we know the entire plan, nothing happens.

When we commit, then Providence moves, which to me means that God works in our favor and gives us more help and direction, little by little. As the scripture in Isaiah 28: 10 of the Old Testament says, "Precept upon precept, and line upon line, here a little and there a little." All those precepts, those ideas, those lines, and those actions add up, little by little, revealing to us each step we should take.

In my case, as I took my husband's advice to heart, I was able to move forward with developing Becoming Threads. His words have helped me have the courage to take action in many areas of my life. They are what have allowed me to focus on moving forward rather than worrying about everything I don't know how to do.

J. K. Rowling, the author of the *Harry Potter* series, has said, "We do not need magic to change the world, we carry all the power we need inside ourselves already: we have the power to imagine better." As I have taken *action* by first choosing positive and uplifting words to think, my feelings about stepping forward to do difficult things have changed. I have discovered the power to imagine better. I have learned that I have the power to create already inside me. I have discovered that each step leads to the next, and the "how" is revealed *in the doing*.

If I hadn't taken the first steps to launch my T-shirt business and waited until I was "educated" enough to justify the risk involved, I would still be sitting around talking about it. As I moved forward, more questions came up, and one by one, they were answered for me. Then more was revealed as I stepped closer to living my true desire. Applying each of the Power Words in any given situation, depending on where I am in the Word Effect cycle, has helped me make so much progress until I have reached the point in many situations where I can now act much more quickly than I have in the past, overcoming fear, avoidance, inertia, and procrastination much more efficiently!

Step 4: Keep It Simple by Setting Small, Measurable Goals

As you take steps toward achieving your goals and discover how along the way, I also invite you to keep things simple. This principle has been key to my finding the courage to begin new or daunting tasks. I am good at taking an idea and then thinking myself right out of it—let's face it, most of us are! Fear of the unknown, of failure, of what other people will think are real concerns that many of us face each day. But I have learned to manage those fears by keeping things straightforward and uncomplicated and by using the power of words to combat any feelings that don't serve me.

To keep the process simple, I encourage you to set small, measurable goals and be sure to establish your own boundaries. A friend and mentor of mine, Connie Sokol, calls these small goals "chewable chunks." I remind myself constantly that I don't have to do everything today . . . I just need to have a desire to do something. Success comes when I honor the commitments I have made to myself.

Connie mentored me with the writing of the first draft of this book and would sometimes say, "Get your bum in the chair and write." My commitment to writing every day for twenty-five minutes was so important for me to keep. When I sat down to write, I eliminated all distractions, including my phone. I set an alarm and began to write. I wrote when I wanted to and, more importantly, wrote when I *didn't* want to. I actually scheduled the time on my calendar and honored that commitment. It was a simple approach, and it worked! If someone needed something from me at the time I was supposed to be writing or if doing something else seemed more appealing, I would remind myself that I had made this commitment to myself and that I needed to take care of it first before doing anything else.

The following experience is the perfect illustration of why it's important to break things down into small, manageable, "chewable chunks." Several years ago, our garage became full of some personal belongings of a person who had recently passed away. I kept waiting for the perfect weekend wherein I could devote six to eight hours to go through everything and get my garage back to where I could park in it. The weeks kept passing by, and I would always look to the next Saturday with anticipation that this would be the day to accomplish my goal. But as the week progressed, other responsibilities and distractions would get in the way, affecting the time I had on Saturday to get anything of any significance done. Before I knew it, the day had eroded away. This cycle led to frustrating feelings that stemmed from thoughts about how there just wasn't enough time to get the project done.

As I was discussing my frustrations with a dear friend, she wisely offered me a suggestion. "How about setting the timer for thirty minutes and going out in your garage every day while the kids are in school?" she offered. "Then start working on tidying up whatever you can in that half hour. When the timer rings, you can decide if you want to do thirty more minutes or if you are done for the day. Don't do more than an hour . . . even if you want to. Go through what you can, and when the timer goes off, be done for that day." She told me I would be amazed at how much I got done over a week or two's time if I tried this method. "When your car becomes full of stuff to donate or take to the dump," she advised, "take it right then. Finish the first task you begin before moving on to something else. Over time," she promised, "you will see something happening!"

Her suggestions have worked incredible power in my life to act and move forward. Simply setting a timer and doing a little work each day has been life-changing. Often, when the timer went off, I would want to keep going, partly because I felt the pressure to do more. Progress had been slow in the beginning, and my brain often questioned how I might accomplish the big goal.

But as I practiced constraint to keep from going longer than I had committed and showed up each day to honor the commitment I had made to myself, something did indeed happen. After a few weeks, the project was almost complete! By taking things just thirty minutes at a time, the project felt much more manageable and less overwhelming. I simply heeded the age-old advice we've all heard: *How do you eat an elephant? Why, one bite at a time, of course!*

Consistency Is Key

I've known for a long time that being consistent is crucial when it comes to taking *action*, but I have come to realize it might just be the most important thing—the key to *everything else* falling into place! The start-stop approach is the undoing of so many well-laid plans. When you understand how important it is to not only take action but remain consistent in it, everything will fall into place for you too.

Jerry Seinfeld is one of the most successful comedians of all time and the perfect example of the power that consistent effort can have in life. As a kid, I grew up watching the *Seinfeld* TV series—a show "about nothing" where Jerry Seinfeld plays a semi-fictionalized version of himself. The show, which Seinfeld not only acted in but wrote and directed, was hugely popular during its ten-year run and remains so today.

According to *Forbes*, Jerry Seinfeld made $267 million in 1998 (at the peak of his sitcom's run), and in 2008, he was still pulling in $85 million a year. By popularity, wealth, and critical acclaim, Seinfeld had it all. But his success wasn't only because he was a tremendously funny comedian. It was also in large part due to the fact that he was willing to show up, consistently putting in the effort to achieve the desires of his heart.

In an article on his website entitled "How to Stop Procrastination on Your Goals by Using the 'Seinfeld Strategy,'" James Clear, author of *Atomic Habits*, talks more about why Jerry Seinfeld has been so successful for so long. "What is most impressive about Seinfeld's career isn't the awards, the earnings, or the special moments; it's the remarkable consistency of it all. Show after show, year after year, he performs, creates, and entertains at an incredibly high standard. Jerry Seinfeld produces with a level of consistency that most of us wish we could bring to our daily work."

It's easy to look at Seinfeld's success, fame, and fortune and think if we had his luck, talent, and life, we could be successful too. But it isn't just luck that has made Seinfeld a success. "Compare his results to where you and I often find ourselves," Clear goes on to note. "We want to create but struggle to do so. We want to exercise but fail to find motivation. . . . What's the difference?" He goes on to explain that the difference is what some call the "Seinfeld Strategy," wherein Jerry, unlike other comedians, practiced his jokes every day. He was consistent with his work, both on the days he wanted to do it and the days he didn't.

Another article published by Chloe Britton shared this about the Seinfeld Strategy: "In Seinfeld's case, [he wrote] a minimum amount number of jokes daily." She goes on to explain how this "strategy" can be applied by anyone to anything, from work, to exercise, to eating healthy. "It's all in doing, the achieving," Britton says. Each day after achieving his little goal, Seinfeld would mark a big X on his calendar. Day after day, he went about doing the little things, which truly led to very big things for him. "The key is to never break the chain [of doing the little things]," Britton says. "That would leave a gap and mean starting again, and nobody wants to do that." Can you imagine where you might be in just a short time if you take consistent action daily, even on the days when you don't want to?

Darren Hardy, *New York Times* bestselling author, shares how he has found success with his book *The Compound Effect*. "The Compound Effect is the principle of reaping huge rewards from a series of small, smart choices. . . . Habits are that 'compound interest of self-improvement.' If you can get just one percent better at something each day, by the end of a year, you will be 37 times better." I'll admit, improving by only 1 percent each day seems unremarkable at first. But that jump to 37 percent improvement in just a year reflects incredible progress! All it takes is daily, consistent action.

This incremental approach to change, facing our fears, and taking action is inspiring. Taking small steps has especially helped me when my primitive brain has told me I can't do something or don't want to do something. Instead of reasoning out the issue, I quickly decided I could do it anyway by taking the first little bitty step. Expect that your primitive brain is going to tell you why you can't every time you make a choice to act. Coming up with a plan beforehand for taking micro steps will combat those thoughts so you can remain committed to your goal.

Remember, "When you fail to plan, you plan to fail," words often credited to Benjamin Franklin for saying. These simple words are truer than many of us realize. The actions we take or don't take often seem so small. But the power comes by consistently doing those small things, even when we don't see why we should at the moment.

These words from the former president of The Church of Jesus Christ of Latter-day Saints, Howard W. Hunter, are some of my favorites: "True greatness . . . always requires regular, consistent, small, and sometimes ordinary and mundane steps over a long period of time." I have loved putting these words on because I do feel capable of being consistent in doing small, ordinary, and mundane tasks over a long period of time. This is a simple formula for true greatness, and it is within my reach.

One of the best illustrations of the power of taking small steps consistently is the "Magic Penny," as told by Darren Hardy in *The Compound Effect*: "If you were given a choice between taking $3 million in cash this very instant and a single penny that doubles in value every day for thirty-one days, which would you choose?" Of course, my first thought was I would take the $3 million since a penny doubled each day for thirty-one days surely would not come close to $3 million! This seemed like a trick question . . . but was it?

Hardy continues: "If you've heard this before, you know the penny gambit is the choice you should make—you know it's the course that will lead to greater wealth." Yet why is it so hard to believe choosing the penny will result in more money in the end? After all, it's such a small amount, it doesn't seem like it has enough significance to build that much wealth behind it over thirty-one days. It's also hard to believe in the penny because it takes so much longer to see the payoff.

The results are not immediate; they take time. But Hardy then explains what happens with the penny over thirty-one days:

> Let's say you take the cold, hard cash and your friend goes the penny route. On Day Five, your friend has sixteen cents. You, however, have $3 million. On Day Ten, it's $5.12 versus your big bucks. After twenty full days, with only eleven days left in the month, your friend only has $5,243. Then the invisible magic of the Compound Effect starts to become visible. The same small mathematical growth improvement each day makes the compounded penny worth $10,737,418.24 on Day Thirty-One, more than three times your $3 million. In this example, we see why consistency over time is so important. On Day Twenty-nine, you've got your $3 million. [Your friend has] $2.7 million. It isn't until Day Thirty of this 31-day race that the penny pulls ahead, with $5.3 million. And it isn't until the very last day of this month-long ultra-marathon that your friend blows you out of the water.

Are you still scratching your head? Consistency isn't always appealing or easy, but it is so worth it—even with a penny!

Future Focus: The Power That Makes Continual Action Possible

When you fully commit, break tasks into small steps, and act consistently, you can accomplish the desires you set out to achieve. You can even see the beginning of long-term change because you understand how to better confront procrastination and fear each time they arise with each new circumstance you face. But the ability to apply the

Power Word *action* over the long haul—to achieve things you have never tried before and have no evidence you are capable of accomplishing—requires what's called "Future Focus."

What is Future Focus? It has to do with the thoughts you choose to think about things you have never done before. It's how you find the courage to take actions you are totally unfamiliar with. Having a Future Focus means that before the primitive lizard brain even has a chance to stop you with feelings of fear or dread about the unknown, you are already having thoughts that help you feel committed, capable, and confident. A Future Focus means you are constantly looking forward in faith, hope, and joyful anticipation toward the future instead of backward on the failures of the past. This faith in your future self allows you to smack down your past self when you ask your present self to believe you can do something with no evidence from your past to prove you can do it.

Remember the Reticular Activating System (RAS) I mentioned in Chapter 4? It is the RAS's job to always look for evidence to back up what you are thinking. If you are thinking of your past experience, your brain will show you evidence of how you are not prepared to do a new thing because you have never done it before. The brain will have you look to your past for validation of your capability, but this only works if you're looking to accomplish something you have already done in the past. What do you do when you must venture into totally uncharted territory?

Let's take a look at how to create and act using your future self. To illustrate this, I'll use a baby learning to walk as an example. A baby trying to take its first steps has no evidence in its brain that it can walk since the baby has never done it before. If the baby's brain had to hold out for proof from his past that he could walk, he would never learn to walk. All babies learning to walk must put on thoughts from their future selves or remain forever crawling around. This is how a baby learns to do most things—taking small steps, making incremental changes here and there—all based on his future self.

But somewhere, typically in our early adulthood, we stop focusing on our future and begin to focus instead on our past to help us decide what we are capable of. This perspective is very common in most human beings! We begin choosing to think things like, "I've never done it before, so I'm not sure I can do it," or "People have stared at me in the past when I have played the piano, and I'm scared of what they're thinking now." Even though these thoughts seem quite innocent, how do they make you feel? They make me feel insecure. Continually having thoughts like "I've never written a book before" only serves to make me feel totally incapable of writing one since everything from my past seems to prove this point. Instead of taking actions that stem from my future self, I may dwell on my limiting belief and then buffer myself from the feelings of uncertainty and inability with other things to avoid sitting down each day to write.

Without a Future Focus, I may judge myself next to other authors and see how inadequate I am, ultimately putting the manuscript in my closet and deciding the dream was silly. The result I create from the thought, "I've never done it before, so that must mean I can't do it," is continually proving to myself and the world that I am not capable. If I kept thinking like this, I would never finish the book. The negativity bias, which causes our brain to focus on what isn't going right instead of what is, will cause us to stop acting on the desires of our hearts if not redirected.

Here is a list of common limiting beliefs. This list, of course, isn't comprehensive but will give you an idea of how damning such beliefs can be. Are any of these the thoughts you put on regarding the desires of your heart?

- I'm not ready.
- I'm not good enough.
- I'm not creative.
- Who am I to change?
- Why me?
- It has to be perfect.
- I don't know how.
- It is hard.
- I need to compare myself to others.
- I'm too old.
- I'm too young.

If these are the kinds of words you are using to formulate your thoughts, I invite you to let them go and give you permission to discover how to put on new words and thoughts. We *do* have evidence that we can walk, write, or do any number of things we have never done before as we become more aware of our thoughts. If we choose to simply let go of our limiting beliefs and focus on the future instead of what we think we know from the past, we can do anything we set our Future Focus on.

Focusing on the future means you first recognize your limiting beliefs, let them go, and replace them with beliefs that support your dreams. It allows you to get back into the flow of creation. It means focusing on the road ahead instead of focusing on the road behind. To create a different future, you must create something that doesn't exist in your past. You must believe something you don't currently believe. What kind of life you create out of the actions you take is based on the words and thoughts you choose to put on.

This, my friends, is why *words matter*! The words you put on daily not only help you deal with the past and what's happening in the present moment but, most importantly, create your future life. A beautiful life full of purpose and promise is possible only when you choose to put on the focused words that will create that future.

The Power of Commitment, Courage, Capability, and Confidence

Most people believe that the inspiration, motivation, or enthusiasm they need to take action will just come to them. What they don't realize is that we create inspiration to act with the words we choose to think. Once you understand this, you can take responsibility for the emotional fuel you use to give energy to your life.

Dan Sullivan, founder and president of The Strategic Coach Inc., teaches the four Cs formula: commitment, courage, capability, and confidence. As these four Cs deal with the power of four words, I took notice. Sullivan notes how these four words are the building blocks of growth. "Have you ever wondered why some people are super-achievers and seem to go from success to success while others never seem to get out of the starting blocks?" he asks. "In my 40 years of coaching high-achieving entrepreneurs, I've noticed that they all go through a process to help them break through to the next level of success," which, he explains, is the four Cs Formula.

When I wanted to finish writing this book, the first thing I had to feel was *commitment* toward that goal—I had to get fully into the game. When I feel committed, I take different actions than when I'm undecided. I had to commit to how much time I would spend writing each day to continue forward and not cave into any distractions.

The next thing I had to do to finish writing the book was be *courageous* even when I didn't know what I was doing. This is where I often got stuck. I wanted to see the entire picture of how things were going to unfold before I would have the courage to step forward. Courage, to me, doesn't always feel great. The truth is, courage feels terrible a lot of the time because we are doing things we have never done before, which is *highly* uncomfortable for some of us!

"If a goal is worth accomplishing, if a goal stretches us and expands our potential, then we'll feel uncomfortable as we work toward it," says Brooke Castillo of The Life Coach School. "So, when we look at it this way, discomfort is a sign that we're on the right track. It's a sign that we are growing and expanding, becoming the next best version of ourselves." I used to think that if something felt uncomfortable that I shouldn't try to reach for it, and if I was supposed to be doing it, I would feel good about it all the time. This is flawed thinking.

Most worthwhile pursuits and meaningful goals are often very hard and don't feel the least bit pleasant at times. Knowing there would be discomfort in the process of writing this book and being willing to accept it helped me continue. Instead of feeling fearful and full of procrastination, knowing that things aren't necessarily going to be sunshine and roses every minute of the day has helped me remain courageous in the face of difficulty.

Once you are committed and moving forward with courage, you will discover that you can develop a *capability* for doing things you might have thought impossible in the past. You can take one step forward at a time. And as you become more capable, you will become *confident* with your new skills, which will help you remain consistent in your efforts.

Taking *action* requires commitment, courage, and consistency. Being able to take real action requires that you put on the right words that will form the right thoughts. Those thoughts will give you the inspiring and motivating feelings you need to then take the *actions* that will help you create the life of beauty you were meant to live.

Before you go on to Chapter 7, where we will explore Power Word 6, be sure to complete the following challenge.

Challenge Inaction by Taking Simple Steps Forward

1. Since discomfort is a necessary part of accomplishing your goals, ask yourself if you are willing to feel uncomfortable. Write down your promise to step outside of your comfort zone._____

_____

2. What would it be like if you saw discomfort as a green light instead of a red or yellow light? Write down your impressions. _____

_____

_____

_____

3. List five things you would do if you had no fear you couldn't accomplish them: _____

    _____

    _____

    _____

4. What actions will you take this week to begin accomplishing one thing from the list above? Remember to keep them simple and manageable. _____

    _____

    _____

    _____

5. Use the following statements to perform at least one "thought download" this week. Write the words you used to formulate your thoughts based on these statements here, and then determine whether they are circumstances you have no control over or whether they are your opinions or beliefs that may need changing:

    *   I don't like . . .
    *   I don't want . . .
    *   That won't work because . . .
    *   I've never done it, so . . .
    *   It's his/her fault because . . .

"Every success story started with a decision to try and a commitment to keep going."
—Elle Sommer

CHAPTER 7

APPRECIATE

THE POWER WORD THAT LETS YOU ENJOY THE BEAUTY AND WONDER OF THE JOURNEY

"Appreciation can make a day, even change a life. Your willingness to put it into words is all that is necessary."
—Margaret Cousins

Power Word 6: *Appreciate (verb) – to recognize the full worth of something or someone; or, to increase in number or value.*

March 2020 was a time in most people's lives that will never be forgotten. I remember the first week of that month being at a baseball tournament with my son in Las Vegas and hearing talk of a new viral outbreak in China. There was some apprehension about the virus becoming an issue here in the U.S., but it wasn't slowing me or my family down from our active lives, so I didn't give it too much thought that week.

Then we returned home, and almost overnight, things began to change rapidly in my day-to-day life as the world took on the challenge of COVID-19. Things that had always been a part of my life and that I had taken for granted were no longer there. Not being able to go to church every week or send my kids to school was a new experience for me. I began to worry about how this pandemic was going to affect my life down the road.

In early 2020 I had just started my six-month life coach certification through The Life Coach School and wasn't quite sure how to handle homeschooling my kids while I tried to meet my own educational commitments. I found myself putting on words that have always been easy for me to think: "This is not the plan."

As I began to "wear" these words, the problem seemed to grow. Little did I know that what I thought would be a few weeks of online school would stretch on for the rest of the year while I tried to complete my own training from home. Managing my fears of the unknown became harder to do as I waited uncertainly in line just to get into a grocery store and then faced empty shelves once I got inside. At times I wondered what country I was living in, it all felt so strange. It wasn't until the abundance of choices was taken away that I stopped to appreciate how amazing it had been to have all those options around me virtually every day.

As time went on, I began to feel more and more anxious, overwhelmed, and fearful. I will never forget one afternoon six days into the nationwide shutdown when I was alone in my kitchen, getting ready for dinner. I prayed for assurance that everything was going to be okay. I have already shared how God speaks to me in words, often reminding me of phrases or words as if I hear myself saying them. As I have become more aware of the power of words, I have learned how to listen to the way He speaks these words to my heart.

In that moment of mounting despair, the words from a little sign on my bathroom vanity came to me: "All you have is all you want." These words brought comfort to my soul. The circumstances of life didn't change right then as I continued to prepare dinner, but almost instantly, I began to appreciate the things I did have in my life at that very moment. The power to *appreciate* brought me back into the present moment and away from the unknown.

As I began to appreciate all I had, my thoughts changed, and within a few minutes my heart was filled with gratitude and love. That simple phrase from the plaque in my bathroom became a power statement that carried me through many days in 2020. Though life was full of uncertainty, I was grateful that all my children were safe and healthy, my married son and his cute wife had everything they needed up north in their house, my husband was still able to work, I was able to continue my education through virtual means, and we had stocked up our food storage a few weeks before the crisis hit. My pantry and fridge were full, and I didn't "need" anything. On top of that, I truly had all that I wanted as well! The power of words, starting with the Power Word *appreciate*, helped me redirect my perspective to focus on the good.

One of my mentors, Laurel Dawn Huston from Reflections Inside and Out Mentoring Group, said this about the word *appreciation* in a recent post on Facebook: "Appreciation is . . . an ability to understand the worth, quality, or importance of something." Laurel then encourages us to ask ourselves this question: "Look at the scenario and say, what about this [situation] happened *for* me instead of *to* me?" Questions like this can get us out of a fearful state and back into a place of curiosity, where we are freer to appreciate rather than worry about what we think we lack. Even though the problems of 2020 lasted much longer and had a much more significant impact than at first anticipated, I discovered how to appreciate what happened *for* me during this time instead of focusing on what was happening *to* me.

You're likely very familiar with this sense of the word *appreciate* as I've been using it so far. But *appreciate* has another meaning, which is when something gains more value than it had before. My theory is that as we appreciate (or recognize the value in) the things in our lives, those things then appreciate (or gain more and more value). As I look back now, I see how *appreciating* the tender mercies of God helped me become the person I am today, but I also see how those treasured blessings are appreciated in value. I discovered what mattered most as our family developed a closeness we had not had before. My husband and I appreciated our home, our health, and our relationships so much more, and as we appreciated them, they appreciated. The value of what mattered to us most grew and grew.

Like me, I'm sure that 2020 and the months that have followed that stressful year have been filled with anxiety at times for you. But I'm willing to wager that life is getting better and will continue to improve for you and your family, especially as you continue to *appreciate* all you have been blessed with. As you do so, you will be able to keep the momentum of the Word Effect going in your life, even if life seems to be at a standstill at times. That's why *appreciate* is Power Word 6 in the Word Effect cycle of becoming and one that will allow you to climb upward and forward as your practice putting it on.

Appreciation *opens the way to living joyfully in the moment. It creates curiosity where there once was fear. And most of all, it allows you to accurately judge the relationships, circumstances, and emotions of your life, leaving you free to enjoy fully the beauty and wonder of your journey.*

Although the Power Word *appreciate* may seem similar to the Power Word *abundance*, I'd like to make an important distinction between the two. Remember from Chapter 5 that *abundance* taught us to see the good we have in our lives and believe that there is truly enough good out there in the world for all of us. In fact, the more we focus on the good, the more goodness comes into our lives, and the more we can share it with others. *Appreciation*, however, is more than just focusing on the blessings we have. It is about accurately perceiving and respecting the different aspects of our life, whether those be our relationships, our circumstances, or our emotions.

Throughout the remainder of this chapter, I want to show you how to understand what the word *appreciation* really means and how to apply it to the Word Effect cycle so you can continue moving forward along the path of self-discovery and self-mastery. To do this, let's first review all the Power Words in the Word Effect cycle we have covered so far, how they build upon each other, and how *appreciation* fits into the cycle with each of these Power Words.

First, when you *acknowledge* (Power Word 1) where you are and what you want, you naturally begin to *ask* questions (Power Word 2); you begin to be more curious. As you *accept* (Power Word 3) where you are right now, without demanding that life unfold on your terms, you also approach things with an *abundant* heart (Power Word 4). Then you can take steps forward to *act* (Power Word 5) on your personal desires. Once you are acting—moving forward, as it were—the only way to remain on that upward-and-forward-moving trajectory is to *appreciate* (Power Word 6) where you have been and all you have learned. Appreciating allows you to remain committed and stay focused on the goodness and beauty you're discovering and experiencing—to refuse to backslide when times get tough, keep courage alive when fear comes knocking at your door, and refuse to judge life anxiously. Appreciation is the propeller that keeps you moving toward becoming your most beautiful self as you create the kind of life you were always meant to live.

Appreciation Helps You Live Joyfully in the Moment

Applying the Power Word *appreciate* begins when you choose to focus on finding joy in the present instead of worrying about either your past or future. Just like me and just about any other human, I'm sure you have found it so much easier to focus on yesterday or tomorrow instead of raising your gaze to *appreciate* today. We often struggle with this perspective when the suffering starts, or when our focus is downward.

Life goes in only two directions: upward or downward. We rarely stay in one place for very long, so it is up to you and me to decide which way we are going to travel through the choice of words we put on each day. As you put on the Power Word, *appreciate,* you will learn to keep your focus upward on your joyful present. Appreciation will act as part of your compass while you navigate your beautiful life, despite what obstacles come your way.

So just how do you keep your focus on the joyful present? After you have decided to put on the Power Word *Appreciate*, what keeps you in the Word Effect cycle day by day? Just understanding something intellectually isn't necessarily going to motivate you to make it happen. I'm sure you know you should "live in the present." That makes sense, yet that knowledge is not enough. You must learn *how* to live now in your beautiful life. The process can be different for each of us, yet one thing is universal, and that's the need for daily, simple reminders. Let's now consider how you can be reminded each day to *appreciate* all the good in your life.

Become Aware of Your Personal Self-Worth

The first way to sharpen your focus on your present life and all the joy you can experience is to become *aware* of who you really are. We often confuse who we are with what we do, so sometimes, this shift can only happen when what we do is taken away. Have you ever had something taken away from you, and you suddenly realized you didn't appreciate it until it was gone? Mike Robbins, the author of the book *Focus on the Good Stuff*, gives a powerful example of how he learned his true worth when he lost his professional baseball career.

Mike grew up playing baseball and got drafted by the New York Yankees right out of high school, but he didn't play for the Yankees because he got an opportunity to play for Stanford University. He was later drafted by the Kansas City Royals. Once he signed that professional contract, he had to work his way up through the minor leagues to make it to the majors. During his third season with the Kansas City Royals, Robbins threw a pitch that tore a ligament in his elbow and blew his arm out. "So just like that, after starting baseball when I was seven, my career ended," says Robbins. "Now, as you can imagine, I was pretty devastated. When the reality of the fact that my baseball career was over finally set in, I started to ask myself over and over again, *did I have any regrets?* And you know what was interesting, I didn't regret a lot of the stuff I thought I would have. The only regret I had was that I didn't fully appreciate [playing] while it was happening. I was too busy trying to make it."

Too busy making it happen? This was how I had lived much of my life until I discovered the power of the word *appreciate*. When we try to make something happen in our life, we often find ourselves white-knuckling through with teeth gritted, using our willpower to force things along. But at the end of the day, it doesn't matter what we accomplish; it will never be enough because we *haven't learned to appreciate who we are already.*

Mike Robbins notes in his book that part of his problem in not being able to appreciate what he had was that he was always using baseball to make up for feeling inadequate. "I was a kid from Oakland, California, raised by a single mom who didn't have a lot of money and always wanted to grow up and make it to the major leagues and be someone important." This feeling of "unimportance" no doubt stemmed from Robbins not really defining what it meant to have value.

Importance means different things to each of us. When we use vague words, they can cause us to feel like we aren't enough. That feeling leads us to hustle and push to try to prove to ourselves that we are enough. And we can never win with this game plan. All the pushing, shoving, hustling, and forcing prevent us from ever seeing that as sons and daughters of a Divine Creator, we are enough just the way we are. When you stop to *appreciate* who you are and experience the beauty of what you have already accomplished, you become keenly aware of life as it really is—and thankfully, that it is enough for today.

When Mike Robbins couldn't play baseball anymore, he suddenly became aware of all that he *already* was, that he was enough, that he didn't need to prove himself anymore through playing baseball. It wasn't until baseball was taken away that he was finally *aware* of and could appreciate his life for what it was.

As Mike became aware of the power *appreciation* could have in his life, he said he became "fascinated with the idea of how appreciation impacted relationships and teams." He now speaks about the simple concept of appreciation to companies and businesses all over the world. In his research, he has found that not only does appreciation impact relationships and how we feel about ourselves but also our productivity, citing a study by the U.S. Department of Labor that claims the number one reason people quit their jobs is that they don't feel appreciated or valued.

But so often, we tie being appreciated to what we have accomplished and not to who we already are as a person. How often do you focus on being a human *doer* rather than a human *being*? If your focus is on the doing, you will always feel that you have fallen short. Being aware of who you are, where you've been, what you've learned, and all that you have been blessed with is the authentic way we head toward the beautiful life we are meant to lead—all the rest is just an exercise in futility.

When I turned forty-six on November 10, 2021, I learned even more acutely how wonderful life can be when we become more aware of our own goodness as well as that of others. Though this personal experience is nothing you'd find on the news or social media, the significance of the word *appreciate* and how it made me aware of the good in my own life is unforgettable for me.

Two of my boys at this time were serving missions for The Church of Jesus Christ of Latter-day Saints, one in Iowa and the other in Honduras. Missionaries for my church leave the comforts of home for two years to go out and share a message of hope and goodness about Jesus Christ with others. For most of that time, most of their contact with home and family is limited to a brief weekly email or a phone call on a certain day of the week. Yet, on special days, such as their mom's birthday, they are able to make additional calls home.

When I woke up that morning and looked at my messages on Facebook, my heart was filled with joy when I saw that each of my missionary boys had not only sent me birthday greetings but wondered when they could call me to tell me "Happy Birthday" over the phone. We set up a time for later that afternoon, and my whole family (all five boys, my daughter-in-law, and my husband) jumped on a group call. One by one, they extended birthday wishes but also expressed their gratitude for me as their mom. It was the most memorable part of my day, and every time I think of it, I am more keenly aware of the love I am surrounded by and the worth I hold by just being Becky. This simple call was more powerful than any monetary gift my family could have given.

As my family put on the Power Word *appreciate* and offered it to me, it allowed me to recognize that I have inherent value and can find joy in the present moment. Even though I have been far from a perfect mother and have made (and continue to make) mistakes along the way, I have done my best to teach, love, and nurture my children, and my boys appreciate me for that. Feeling appreciated by them caused me to want to continue developing an even more meaningful and loving relationship with each member of my family. It inspired me to continue following the Word Effect cycle upward and forward.

Shift Your Perspective to the Present

The second thing you can do to apply the Power Word *appreciate* in your life is to look for ways to shift your perspective to the present. I learned how to do this on my daily morning walks. I will never forget the morning I realized that as I walked I always looked at the ground. Even though I was out in nature and doing something I truly enjoyed, I stared almost constantly at the pavement in front of my feet. My thoughts focused down as well, lingering on my past and future cares—motherhood, trying to be a good wife, all the to-dos, and even the secret desires of my heart I wanted to explore. I often found myself dwelling on all the things I hadn't gotten done. Sometimes I would finish my walk feeling more burdened than before I walked out the door.

One day as I walked, I had this divine thought come to me: "Becky, practice looking up!" These powerful words from God were quiet and still, yet I heard them deep within me. So, I began to look up and out as I walked, and these early morning strolls began to change. I appreciated the beauty of my neighbor's flowers, the blossoms on the trees, and the falling of the leaves in autumn time. I noticed the sun coming up over the beautiful Wasatch Mountain Range and the variety of clouds and color of the sky. I had never noticed all this beauty and wonder until I began to look up and out, experiencing the world around me in real-time. Shifting my perspective to the present moment has made such a difference for me.

The path I took when I walked didn't change, and the worries on my mind and in my heart didn't disappear suddenly. Yet just looking upward and outward shifted my perspective from the limiting view of what can be seen on the ground to the expansive view that fills the landscape and the sky. My thoughts (and the words I put on) during my walks have been revamped, and this in turn has allowed me to feel differently. The positive feelings I experience then affect the actions I take and what kind of life I create for myself. And all this from a simple shift in perspective—from moving my focus from the ground to the sky and the nature present around me.

As I began to look up and out on my walks, I realized that in one stretch of the course I took, a gradual elevation change prevented me from seeing the entire stretch from one end to the other until I had walked it step by step. As I noticed this, I had another divine "download" reminding me that on the path of life, we must take just one step at a time. If we don't look up and appreciate what is here and now, we will miss the little things, the things that have the power to shift our perspective, to see things more clearly, to assign a more accurate weight to the matters in our lives, to experience the present moment with joy. This simple reminder stays with me each day now and as I go out. I walk with my shoulders back and look up and out at what is right before me, *appreciating* the good and savoring the beautiful.

Another way to achieve this shift in perspective is to look at how a lack of appreciation affects the lives of others. Following is an experience I had that helped me see what happens when we choose not to look for the good in others and instead focus on perceived problems.

One Sunday morning some time ago, I went to choir practice looking forward to learning the songs for an upcoming Christmas program. The music was beautiful, the surroundings were peaceful, and there was so much to be grateful for as a group of us joined to raise our voices in praise to God. Within the first few minutes, however, I noticed that the lady sitting next to me was looking at her phone and audibly sighing with frustration. I began to feel the energy surrounding me shift from a positive and beautiful vibe to one of negativity.

She started to mumble things like, "I don't have time for this" and "How is this going to work?" She sighed again and again, shaking her head. Finally, I asked her if she was okay. She looked at me and said, "I have just been asked to attend a meeting later today that I had not planned on and to step in and speak at a function tonight for someone who is sick." My first thoughts were, "That's it? That doesn't seem like a big deal." Of course, I didn't know what was really going on in her life, and it wasn't my job to determine how she should react, but I did think she was getting awfully worked up over an issue I perceived to be quite small.

As choir practice continued, I began to think about how I might have reacted to a similar situation. On my high horse, I thought that I would probably very happily help out with a smile because it would be the "right thing to do" to be willing to serve others at any time. But the truth is, I am a human being, and I often have a day planned with things I want to get done or think I need to get done. When something unexpected comes out of the blue and disrupts my plans, I, too, can stop seeing the good around me and step into suffering instead.

As I have confessed in other chapters, words like "this is not the plan" have frequently come to my mind in the past, which have caused feelings of frustration just like the woman sitting next to me was experiencing. Observing her inability to keep her focus on the beauty of her surroundings, the music we were singing, and the blessing of being there in choir caused me to reflect on my own behavior as I saw what suffering she caused herself by focusing on the negative and her future problems.

I appreciated this little experience of observing her reactions because it helped me to recommit to myself and to God that I want to look for the good in each moment of my day, no matter what happens, and to see the demands on my time as opportunities to serve and help others rather than annoying inconveniences that get in the way of my plans. To *appreciate* and experience the present doesn't mean we always do what we want to do at that moment, but if we pause, take a deep breath, and refocus our hearts on the joy we can find in the present, we can overcome the negativity bias.

Practice, Practice, Practice

The third thing you can do to live in the present, joyful moment is to *practice* being content with what is happening rather than focusing on what isn't. One of the best ways to do this is to keep a gratitude journal. I learned the importance of this activity several years ago when a mentor of mine saw the negativity bias that was running my life and encouraged me to start writing down ten things each night that I was grateful for. She had started this practice herself, and it had made a big difference in her own life, so she shared the idea with me. I didn't appreciate (there's that word again!) the significance of this activity at the time; I almost didn't even hear her words because I was not focused on listening. But I reluctantly agreed to start the gratitude journal.

After day three of keeping the journal, I hadn't seen any big changes in myself, and instead of writing down all the good things that were happening, I slowly began to let the negativity creep back in. Eventually, I stopped writing in my gratitude journal. Three days were not long enough to prove anything—it takes consistent efforts to see any lasting change—but I was ready to move on. As quickly as I had started, I found myself letting other things take precedence or telling myself I was too tired, and what did it matter anyway?

Another couple of months went by, and my mentor kindly asked me if I had ever started the journal. I sheepishly told her that I had done it for about three days and then got distracted. "I didn't see any results, so I quit." I could hear her smile over the phone as she patiently said, "How about you try starting it again and give it some time? Commit to writing in it every day both when you want to and even when you don't want to." Hearing her kind words sparked enough curiosity in me to start again, so I began writing, and this time I committed to myself that I would be as consistent as possible. I wrote in my gratitude journal when I wanted to, and more importantly, I mustered the energy to write when I didn't want to. I was feeling committed this time because I consciously put on the thought, "I am capable of writing down ten things I am grateful for each day and letting go of the results." Each night I wrote ten things. It required a bit of effort, in the beginning, to come up with that number, but it helped me focus on the good I'd experienced throughout my day.

After a while, I noticed that I was focusing more on the present joy in my life and putting on words that better served me. I began to feel different, better than I had in a long time. Nothing changed with the circumstances in my life, but my eyes opened to all I had in the present moment instead of all I'd been worrying about in my past and future.

In his book *Aspire*, Kevin Hall writes, "It's been said that vision is what we see when we close our eyes. We have to see it before we can be." For me to experience joy in my everyday moments, I had to start by writing my appreciation down on paper. I had to practice getting it out, and then I could see it and focus my mind there.

I was training my brain to appreciate the present. And remember, whatever we appreciate . . . appreciates! The more I practiced looking for the good each day through this journal, the more I saw it. My life was amazing, and the only things that changed were the words I was focusing on.

Appreciation Lets You Be More Curious and Less Fearful

The Power Word *appreciate* abolishes fear. It helps you become more open and curious and less closed and withdrawn. As you appreciate more about your life, you will be able to keep the momentum of the Word Effect going, which will create a natural curiosity about the world and all it has to teach you. This allows you to climb upward even when adversity strikes.

As a life coach, I teach that life is fifty-fifty—there is always going to be opposition and resistance when we attempt to move forward. That's just part of life. The trick is to practice *appreciating* the good despite the things we don't like. I'm sure that just like me, the hardest moments in your life are the character-building moments that cause you to focus on the good and learn from the hard. If you never have an overcast or rainy day, you will stop appreciating the blue-sky-and-sunshine days.

One way to deal with adversity is to be curious about what you can learn from it rather than fearing what it might "do to you" or how it will disrupt your plans. See if this illustration of the principle in the following scenario resonates with you.

Let's say you and your family are traveling from Salt Lake City to Disneyland (better known as "The Happiest Place on Earth"). You have decided to travel by car and are loaded up with everything you might possibly need for the seven-hundred-mile trip. You begin your travels excitedly and anticipate the wonderful time you and your family will soon be having. You quickly discover, however, that the journey is where the real experience is.

First, one of your children is touching another child, and they fight and bicker. You must decide how you're going to react to this—with either anger and frustration or calm and patience. Then everyone needs multiple bathroom breaks, which only extends your time on the road and takes away from the "real" vacation you are looking forward to. Then there's "I'm hungry" and "When will we be there" coming from the back seat, and the frustration mounts for Mom and Dad up front. All your plans for the "perfect" trip begin to fade away.

After driving for several hours, everyone seems to have settled in, and things are quiet. Suddenly you hear a loud pop and realize you have just blown a tire. "Are you kidding me?" you say to yourself. "Of all the times to have this happen!"

You pull off to the side of the road and start to look for the best solution to the problem. It doesn't take too long to put on the spare and then head to the nearest tire store to get a new one, but the failed tire and mishap were not in the plan. This unanticipated detour again brings some frustration. You think to yourself, "This is not on my agenda!"

Finally, you have a new tire and are ready to get back on the road again. Your dream of the perfect vacation, so meticulously planned out and anticipated, has not gone how you wanted. What do you do now? Do you turn around and go home? NO! You start where you are and continue moving forward. After all, you didn't have to turn around and go home to get the tire fixed. You fixed it *where you were*, and then you adjusted your plan and continued working toward your anticipated larger goal.

As each event unfolds on your journey, you must remember that you have little control over most of what happens. Through all this, time keeps ticking by, minute by minute. You have a choice: you can either be anxious and upset that things aren't "going right," or you can learn to be in the moment and *appreciate* and learn from what is happening right then. You can be curious about life as it unfolds right at that moment and drops back into wonder instead of worry.

A simple saying often shared in twelve-step recovery programs is, "Don't quit before the miracle." I often reflect on these words when I notice that I am focused on the end result rather than on the journey. When unexpected misadventures arise, I ponder what I can learn and appreciate from them. When I do, I often find a miracle waiting for me on the other side; I find change, I find wonder, I find joy.

The mishaps of living never seem to ask to come during a convenient time—they come on life's terms, not ours. This is why discovering the Power Word *appreciate* is so vital to living a life of joy. In every obstacle, we need to practice pausing, taking the time to be curious (and not furious), and resisting the urge to react in haste. When we do, we can learn that a solution is available. None of us will reach our goals and dreams without staying engaged, in the game, and curious about what we might learn. We can't give in to fear and give up. Giving up is the worst thing we can do! We must resist the urge to "turn around and go home."

As I have become more *appreciative* of what is happening right now and less concerned about where I had planned to go, I have been blessed with a greater sense of wonder about life. I now enjoy a delightful anticipation about the world and what I might learn, how I might grow, and even how much more I will receive by letting life flow rather than demanding it go the way I insist it should. This attitude has helped do away with a lot of fear and anxiety and made me more childlike, and excited about the future rather than dreading what might happen in it. It has made me appreciate the people in my life more, even when some of their behavior has been difficult or unwanted. It has made me more hopeful and less discouraged. And it has helped me appreciate so much more of what God has given me and yet waits to give me.

As you put on the Power Word *appreciate*, you will see that it is up to you to choose how you spend your time. Whether it is filled with affliction or ease, you must choose to love the little things in life—the little moments that seem insignificant until you look back on them and realize how consequential they truly were. You will see how *appreciation* lets you feel childlike wonder about what is unfolding on your journey. To truly enjoy the wonder of your journey, you must learn to appreciate your time and spend it wisely.

Appreciate Your Time

We all have the same amount of time: twenty-four hours in a day and one hundred and sixty-eight hours in a week. Do you appreciate that time? There is no way to create more time—believing that we can have more than we do is a false construct that we, as humans, have set up and based our lives around. The fact is we do not control time. What we can do is *appreciate* what time we do have and not try to overschedule it or cram too much into it. If you don't appreciate the time, it won't appreciate you and give you the ability to achieve your most cherished dreams.

The way you spend your time has to do with how you feel, and your feelings are brought on by your thoughts, not your circumstances. If you are not getting the results you want with the time you have, you have the power to change this. It has to do with the words you choose to think.

I appreciate the simple things today because I have allowed myself time to do so. As you remember to *appreciate* your time and become more intentional in how you spend it, it will naturally appreciate. One of my favorite speakers, Dieter F. Uchtdorf of the Quorum of the

Twelve Apostles of The Church of Jesus Christ of Latter-day Saints, said some words in his 2010 General Conference talk that have stuck with me and helped me keep an appreciation of time:

> *"If life and its rushed pace and many stresses have made it difficult for you to feel like rejoicing, then perhaps now is a good time to refocus on what matters most. . . . When stress levels rise, when distress appears, when tragedy strikes, too often we attempt to keep up the same frantic pace or even accelerate, thinking somehow that the more rushed our pace, the better off we will be."*

This need to rush, to push the pace, to fail to pause and reflect and to be curious rather than reactive when times get tough, is one of the biggest traps I have found myself in over the years of hurry, hustle, and willpower. I have often found myself thinking that if I just had more time, then I could live the life I desired. In the past, I saw the trouble as a time problem, not a mind problem. I would muster up all the willpower I had to push through the day-to-day and always lose because it didn't matter how much I accomplished; I couldn't *appreciate* it. I always focused on what I didn't get done. If I had a to-do list of ten things for that day and I accomplished eight instead of all ten, I focused on what wasn't done rather than appreciating all the good I had managed to make happen.

"Let's be honest, it's rather easy to be busy," Uchtdorf continues.

> *"We all can think up a list of tasks that will overwhelm our schedules. Some might even think that their self-worth depends on the length of their to-do list. They flood the open spaces in their time with lists of meetings and minutia—even during times of stress and fatigue. Because they unnecessarily compli-*

*cate their lives, they often feel increased frustration, dimin-
ished joy, and too little sense of meaning in their lives."*

Think for a moment about your own schedule and whether you appreciate your time or abuse it. Are you grateful for what time you do have,
or are you pushing through with sheer willpower and never feeling
like you have enough hours in the day? If you are constantly rushing,
I urge you to slow down, take a deep breath, and be more reflective in
your approaches to what you want to accomplish each day.

Choose Better How You Will Spend Your Time

When I put on one of my 'Becoming Threads' shirts, they help me
spend my time more wisely. The words not only help me as I go
throughout my day, but I have learned they help others as well with
what words they will choose to think. This will, in turn, affect the way
they feel, which will ultimately determine how they choose to spend
their time and what kind of life they will live that day. Each time I
walk by a mirror or notice what I am wearing, those words act as a
reminder: "Oh yes, this is what I choose to spend my time working
on today."

And I love that my focus on a certain word is *just for that day.* When I
work on improvement in any area of my life, taking small and simple
steps feels more manageable and doable. Worrying about applying
those words to my thoughts for the rest of my life is too overwhelming. But today I can choose to use the time within it to put on a Power
Word that keeps me moving upward and forward.

One of the most powerful tools in addiction and recovery programs
is the idea of trying something one day at a time. In the past, when

I balked at the idea of being able to overcome food addiction for the rest of my life and wanted to run away, my sponsor asked me this simple question: "Would you be willing to try it just for today?" When she suggested this approach, my brain was able to relax a bit, and I could commit to using the next twenty-four hours to try. "I might not do it tomorrow or the next day, but for today, I will try," I would think.

Breaking down hard things into manageable chunks throughout my day has allowed me to make changes in my personal life, taking consistent steps forward one day at a time. Realizing I have choices has made all the difference and has been a huge miracle in my own life. As John C. Maxwell, *New York Times* bestselling author, coach, and speaker, has said, "Life is a matter of choices, and every choice you make makes you." This simple approach to life allows me to appreciate that I have the power to choose how I will use my time each and every day, which in turn allows me to enjoy the journey more.

As most people know, the 2020 Summer Olympics held in Tokyo had to be postponed a year due to COVID-19 and were held in 2021 instead. Can you imagine being all ready to compete in 2020 and then being told you had to wait another year, stay at your best athletic ability, remain healthy, avoid injury, and be happy about this? That thought would make me feel overwhelmed, confused, and discouraged, to say the least. But after watching the Olympics in 2021, I believe the athletes that decided to continue to work on their dream—showing up day after day to practice and disciplining themselves for the additional year—were able to do this because of the little ways they had chosen to spend their time along the way. Their appreciation of the time they had made all the difference when it came time for the big moment of competition. It is in the little things, the daily moments where we choose to show up and put on words, that keep us committed and allow us to achieve the bigger goal.

In an article in *Sports Illustrated*, Pat Forde, the father of Olympic swimmer Brooke Forde, recounts his experience watching his daughter be awarded the Silver Medal in Tokyo. Even though this was a big moment for her, it was the little moments he observed all along the way to her becoming an Olympic champion that made all the difference. "Moments like that [his daughter winning the Silver], it's so much fun . . . but moments at [training] camp are where we become Team USA," said Forde. "It's the . . . little moments—it's not the big moments that are caught on camera. It's the moments you don't see. The phrase 'little moments' made me realize—they actually are the big moments."

It seems each one of us has little moments each day, and if we don't take the time to *appreciate* them and choose to use what time we have wisely, we will never appreciate the joy of living. It is often easier to notice the little moments in other people's lives but forget that we are having little moments, too. An unknown author has said, "Appreciate life as it happens. Moments will soon pass and you will wish you had treasured them more." Don't wait to "live" only for the big moments; choose to see value in all your time, even the seemingly little things.

Appreciation Leaves You Free to Be Your Best Self

As appreciation helps you live in the moment, it also (most importantly) lets you accurately judge your relationships, circumstances, and emotions so you can freely become your best self and let others be their best as well. I love this quote by the late Brigham Young University-Idaho music professor, Newel Kimball, which I think perfectly explains the freedom gratitude gives us to be our best selves, helping us accurately judge our relationships and circumstances rather than condemning them for not being enough:

> Apparently, God expects us to accept everything with a sense of thankfulness: for life itself; the eternal nature of the soul and all that pertains to the maintenance, enjoyment, and continuance of it; the beauty surrounding us everywhere; the aromas; the colors; the food; revealed science and technology; travel; animals; people; the senses that perceive all of it; the memory; expectations; precious relationships. All of it. By exercising the will to be grateful, we lose the will to judge and condemn. We cease being a victim. We cease blaming others and God for everything we dislike because there is so little to dislike. We see the power behind forgiveness and the beginning of acceptance.

This ability to more accurately see ourselves and others is a powerful and wondrous gift from applying the Power Word *appreciate* to your life. I can say this with confidence because this is what this Power Word has done for me. Let's talk more about how *appreciating* helps us refrain from judging and condemning, playing the victim, or needlessly blaming those around us.

Appreciation Before Judgment

During my first year of coaching, I decided to organize a mastermind women's group which I entitled "Certain Women." I'd had several ideas about this group and waited and waited for clarity until I realized that the "how" would be revealed in the doing. So, I began organizing the content one day at a time and inviting women to join.

We began meeting with ten people (including myself) and finished up thirteen weeks later. What happened along the way was much different than I had anticipated in the beginning, but in many ways, it ended up better than I could have expected.

When this mastermind class was complete, I met with my coach to process what I had learned and what I wanted to do to move forward. I will never forget the wise counsel she gave me. She encouraged me to *first* focus on what went well—to draw my gaze and attention to the things that I thought were positive. She told me to write them down and not just keep them in my head. *Second*, she told me to ask myself what could be improved, and if I knew how to improve it, what would I do? She emphasized the importance of starting with what went well first, putting my focus on the good and allowing me to see and appreciate the positive *before* judging where I might need to make changes.

This exercise was life-changing for me. Now, before I act on anything (e.g., relationships, work issues, my own feelings), I first appreciate everything about the situation, which most certainly affects the way I judge that situation. Once I have truly *appreciated* the good in the situation, then I can ask what may need to change or improve. This concept is vital and bears repeating:

> *Once we have* **appreciated** *the good in any given situation, then we can ask what may need to change or improve.*

Upon exercising such gratitude, I have sometimes found that I am surprisingly content with what is, that nothing needs to be "fixed" or changed or improved—that I am perfectly happy. I then take a minute to write my thoughts down (gratitude journals are a good place for such thoughts). Where improvement does need to be made, I am better able to judge what that change should be because I can more accurately see things for what they truly are. Negativity evaporates quickly, discontentment floats away, and greater feelings of love and peace accompany any work that needs to be done to improve, fix, or change something.

Of course, there is usually always the need for change and improvement because we are fallible humans who are works in progress, but as the quote by Newel Kimball states, "appreciating everything as God expects us to do *first* helps us stop being so harsh in our judgment of life and allows us to be more content." I invite you to appreciate the simple things first and allow yourself the time to do so. Celebrate the good, then choose what you would like to change.

Living in the Right Frame of Mind

Applying the Power Word *appreciation* makes it so much easier to live in the right frame of mind—the place where we experience more clarity of thought, more realistic expectations of ourselves and others, and more peace! Prosperity coach Allyson Chavez has taught me much about how to find success in life without having to struggle unnecessarily with inconsequential and childish thought processes. She emphasizes that the mind has two states, the beautiful state and the suffering state, and you can only be in one state at a time. Furthermore, it is only possible to create, accomplish, love, build up, and so forth when you are in the beautiful state.

You can access the beautiful (or positive) state of mind when you use the higher brain functions, including some parts of the limbic system and the prefrontal cortex—where you put your brain to work for you by being resourceful, connecting with a higher power, and successfully reasoning and problem-solving. This frame of mind allows you to assess the world with a more accurate perspective toward people, places, and situations. You experience all sorts of positive feelings when you are in the beautiful state of mind, such as hope, joy, gratitude, appreciation, and compassion. I'm sure you can pinpoint times in your life when you have experienced these feelings—no doubt you were in a beautiful state of mind at the time, and I'm sure it felt wonderful!

The suffering or negative state, on the other hand, is when you are using the lower part of your brain, or the lizard/primitive brain. Here is where you have fight, flight, or freeze responses to things happening around you. Some of the feelings you experience when you are using your lizard brain include stress, anxiety, burnout, disappointment, boredom, and worry.

Where does your mind spend most of its time? Is it in a suffering state or a beautiful state? Of course, we must all deal with adversity and negativity—as has been outlined previously in this chapter—in order to continue to appreciate the positive. But we don't have to get stuck living in the negative and judging everything based on this suffering state of mind. The gateway to a beautiful state is found in the power of *appreciation*. If you don't begin to question your thinking by first exercising the will to be grateful for what is, already, you will remain stuck in a place that often feels like isolation—a personal hell.

Of course, suffering is part of our human experience. It's going to happen to all of us. It has its purpose and is actually very important to our growth and development in this mortal existence. But the truth I have discovered is that the suffering state of mind is meant to be experienced *only as long as you need to learn from it*. It isn't meant to be a continual state of mind. In fact, you can move out of it much quicker than perhaps you think you can. You have the power to do so as you begin to question your thoughts and appreciate where you are today.

I take time each morning to appreciate my life in what I call "quiet time." Here I reflect very intently on all that is good in my life. I start this quiet time with a prayer and then read something uplifting. This grounds me and gives me a place to focus my mind and heart. An inspiring thought I read one morning out of *Twenty-Four Hours a Day* from Hazelden Mediations was this: "Sunshine is the laughter of nature. Live out in the sunshine. The sun and air are good medicine. Nature is a good nurse for tired bodies. Let her have her way with you." Isn't that beautiful? Reflecting and putting on such words often brings me from the suffering state to the beautiful one.

Another day my mind might be redirected to the beautiful state by putting on these words from the Bible in Galatians 5:22: "But the fruit of the Spirit is love, joy, peace, longsuffering, gentleness, goodness, faith." These words and many others I've read day after day act as my compass to keep me moving forward in appreciation of the way things really are around me, allowing me to have joy in the present moment.

The power to *appreciate* helps me live joyfully in the moment, enjoy the wonder of the journey, and remember I have the power to choose what frame of mind I will be in and how I will judge the people, events, and situations of my day. The Word Effect reminds me always that what words I choose to put on daily affect my frame of mind.

Before going on to Chapter 8 and the final Power Word *aspire*, I'd like to challenge you to look at whatever might be keeping you from appreciating where you are *right now*. There is good in all things if you will begin to look for it. When times get tough, or even when life seems to hold little meaning for you, you still have the power to choose what words to think. When you choose to lighten up and appreciate the present instead of focusing on the past or the future, you will be able to better maintain the progress you have already made in applying each of the previous Power Words in the Word Effect cycle. *Appreciation* keeps you moving forward, allowing you to take steps toward becoming your best and most beautiful self.

Challenge: Practice Redirecting Your Mind as You Appreciate the Little Things

1. Start an appreciation/gratitude journal. Write down three to five things you appreciate each day. Here are some thoughts on how to keep it:

    a) You don't need to edit your list; there is no right or wrong answer.

    b) Writing positive ideas can be a simple way to relax at the end of the day and see your life through a softer lens as you focus on the good of right now.

    c) The only requirement for keeping this journal is to become consistent; do this each day. But if you miss a day, refuse to beat yourself up about it! I have missed many days at times, and when this happens, I just start again from where I am. Someday, you'll look back and see the power you gained from starting where you left off.

2. Think about the way you either appreciate time or are a slave to it. Then write down how you spent your time over the last twenty-four hours. Having an awareness of how you have been spending your time will then give you an indication of how you might want to rethink your use of it.

"Life is beautiful. Cherish every moment even if you are stressed or hurt or whatnot.
There's always a tomorrow and it always gets better."
—Ariana Grande

CHAPTER 8

ASPIRE

THE POWER WORD THAT INSPIRES CREATIVITY AND IMAGINATION

"Becoming the person you aspire to be requires that you stop being that old self."
—Joe Dispenza

Power Word 7: *Aspire (verb) – to direct one's hope or ambitions toward achieving something.*

One of my closest friends, Jody, is twenty years older than I am, almost to the date. Our friendship blossomed in the most normal way, but because of the age difference, you might look at us and think we have little in common. Nothing could be further from the truth. I have discovered that God puts certain women in my life to influence and help me as I navigate the ups and downs and all the in-between that life has to offer. Jody is one of those women.

One day Jody taught me a great lesson that has served me well and helped me many times since. I had asked her for advice, and as she shared her own life experience with me, she mentioned one of her favorite sayings: "Be where you are." Although her story is markedly different from my own, this thought was exactly what I needed to hear at the time. The words she offered allowed me to start feeling differently about the situation I found myself in. I can't recall much of the details of that day other than the love she showed me by sharing a little piece of herself and those powerful words: "Be where you are."

Being able to *aspire*, the seventh and final Power Word in the Word Effect cycle, means you believe you're worthy to reach for something better. Believing this, however, is only possible when you are content and at peace with *where you are* right now. The six Power Words you have explored with me thus far all point to the importance of being content with yourself and everything about your life at this moment so you can move upward and forward toward greater growth and progress.

The Word Effect takes shape and will have great power in your life as you examine each new relationship and situation using these Power Words. As you *acknowledge* situations for what they are, *ask* questions about what those relationships or circumstances mean or can teach you, *accept* what you learn about yourself and others from asking those questions, and relate to the people and situations in your life with an *abundant* attitude, take mindful *action* to become, and then *appreciate* fully the present moment, you will finally be ready to *aspire* to more.

If you have tried applying the previous six words in the cycle to various situations and circumstances in your life, you have likely become more content, joyful, and at peace with all that you are and all that is in your life right now. You are more easily and joyfully "being where you are"! You are now more prepared to wisely seek after the most needful and meaningful things in your life. You are ready to spread your wings and direct worthy aspirations toward achieving the life you were always meant to live—a beautiful life full of possibility.

I love what Maya Angelou has said about being content in the moment yet striving for greater possibilities in the future: "Do the best you can until you know better. Then when you know better, do better." These are words that help me *aspire* upward. They also allow me to put on grace when I don't know how to do something. As I discover and learn more, they give me the courage to reach for my highest potential. You, too, are ready now to *aspire* to your full potential.

When you **aspire** *for more, you will better recognize that you are fully in charge of the direction and aim of your own life, which will give you the courage to reach for your highest potential. As you take small, consistent steps forward, you will become more certain of your worth -- making it easier to connect with others rather than compete.* **Aspiring** *to become all that your Creator intended for you gives you the power to create your best and most beautiful life.*

In this chapter, I want to help you understand what it means to aspire, discover your value, and become more certain of your divine potential. As you do so, you will see your life expand before you and more fully grasp that you do, indeed, have the potential to become what you have always desired to be.

Aspiring to Your Highest Potential

Let's begin this process of *aspiring* by first looking back at some of the negative words you might have been using to describe yourself when you first started reading this book (words that I hope you are now putting on less and less). As I coach and mentor, I often work with women who use words such as "stuck" and "unworthy" to describe themselves and the different aspects of their lives, from work, to family, to personal relationships. These are words that conjure up feelings of being "less than" and "not good enough." When we put on these words, we lose sight of our potential.

Can you relate?

I'm sure, like me, you have used these same negative words to describe yourself at times. But as we have discussed previously, these words all come from our negativity bias. When my clients apply each of the Power Words in the Word Effect cycle, they begin to shift their gaze up and out. This changes their perspective and gives them the desire to become a bit more, to *aspire* to live a more joyful life and stop waiting for circumstances around them to change so they can reach their highest potential. For you to truly *aspire*, you must learn to recognize the progress you've already made, remember your value and purpose, guide yourself with the right words, and connect with those around you.

Look How Far You've Come!

One of the best ways to *aspire* to your highest potential is to examine how far you have already come. Recently, I finished up a six-month coaching program with a client and asked her to look back on our time together so, hopefully, she could see just how far she had come. Being able to recognize her own progress, her own value that came through the efforts she made to change, was a wonderful gift I wanted to give her. I have received this gift myself with the guidance of my own coaches and mentors, who helped me see the progress I have made.

With this particular client, I was amazed to see the light in her eyes as she reflected on the way things had transpired over the last six months and realized the growth and expansion she had experienced. She was becoming aware of some real possibilities for her life. I asked her what the word *aspire* meant to her, and she said her focus was finally where it should be—on making progress, not trying for perfection, daring to continue stepping forward and trying again and again to become a bit better every day. It was clear that she was beginning to feel worthy to *aspire* to her highest potential by changing her words, changing her focus, and changing her daily outcomes.

Often you won't see the meaning or effect of the mundane and ordinary steps you take, as we have already seen. It's when you take time to reflect on the journey and look back that you will realize how far you've actually come; that's when you can see the true miracle. I have been surprised by the number of times I have viewed my life in retrospect and thought, "Wow . . . How have I come this far? When did I get here?"

Arriving at that miraculous place of progress and personal development doesn't happen all at once. Improvement is made one step at a time, but that forward movement does take place so long as you are making the effort to try. When you can look back and see how far you've come, you give yourself hope for the future, which spurs you to aspire for more. Reflecting on how far you've come prepares you for the rest of your journey as you recognize your purpose—your value at this very moment, whatever circumstances you may find yourself in.

"Come for Such a Time as This"

Part of *aspiring* to reach your highest potential involves not only seeing where you've been but also the value of who you already are. One of the most beautiful examples of a person who recognized her own value is Queen Esther, whose story is found in the Bible. I love to hear my mother tell that story, which she often got the opportunity to do when she and my dad served as missionaries for The Church of Jesus

Christ of Latter-day Saints at a young women's church camp in Heber City, Utah. My parents supervised a campground called "Esther," named after this queen from the Old Testament.

Hundreds of girls ages twelve to eighteen attended the camp, and as each new group of young women arrived for their week-long experience, my mom told them the story of Queen Esther, a great woman of faith who started out as a young Hebrew girl and later became the queen of Persia because of her beauty. When she realized the chief advisor to her husband, the king, had obtained a decree to put all the Hebrews to death, through great courage, she was able to help her nation. The king was unaware that Esther was Hebrew herself. She revealed her nationality, speaking up at great personal risk, to obtain a decree from her husband to save her people. Though Esther never aspired to this difficult task, when asked to do so, she had the courage to take the next step.

As she put love for herself and others above the fear of losing her life, she took her rightful place as a worthy monarch, a person able to rule over her people with wisdom and compassion—certain of her own value. Speaking of Esther's value and potential to save her people, her uncle declared to her, "Who knoweth whether thou art come to the kingdom for such a time as this?"" (Esther 4:14).

As part of her message at the girls' camp, my mom assured the young women in attendance that each was a modern-day Esther, come or such a time as this. It was vital that each girl aspires to the greatness within her, to see the value and full potential she could read.

As I listened to my mother tell the story of Esther one night at the camp, I realized we have each been sent to earth to fulfill a purpose, just like this amazing woman of the Bible. Perhaps my own mission is to save and protect my family in a time when there is so much chaos in the world. Maybe my purpose is to stand for truth by helping others see that truth more fully through the power of words.

What about you? Do you understand your own value? Have you discovered a purpose based on the special gifts and talents you possess? I invite you now to ask yourself what you are meant to become by examining your own worth. What are you here on this earth to accomplish? If you aren't sure, remember that applying the Power Words in the Word Effect cycle will help you see value in yourself right now ("be where you are") while coming to understand more fully whom you are meant to aspire to become.

Words Can Act as a Compass

As you have seen by now, words can often act as a compass to direct you forward despite the different twists and turns life throws at you, allowing you to *aspire* to greater achievements even in the face of adversity or uncertainty. Words can help you be more aware of your thoughts, which in turn affect your feelings and ultimately direct the outcome of your life. Words, I hope, as they have for me, are helping you become more conscious of how your negativity bias can drag you down and make it impossible to *aspire* to more. Understanding where you are in the Word Effect cycle and living contented in the present is what will allow you to move out of any negativity, behaviors, or thought processes that keep you stuck. Power Words like *aspire* will help you direct all your hopes and ambitions toward living your best and most beautiful life.

Words have the power to bring intention and awareness about your focus and allow you to align with the light within. As you journey through life, these "word compasses" can remain constant, pointing you in the direction you desire to go. The purpose of a compass is to keep you focused on the path you are traveling at all times, keeping you from getting lost. When I was lost in my own life, with all my distracted discontent, putting on the Power Words one at a time is what ultimately helped point me in the right direction and kept me *aspiring* to move upward and forward.

Words keep you heading in the right direction, much like a riverbank guides a river. Think of a river that *isn't* contained by a riverbank: The water in such a river, rather than flowing its course, will simply pool in places. Not moving in any particular direction, the river has no power to refresh the surrounding valleys and plains. When a river runs within a riverbank, however, the water flows exactly where it is intended to go. In the same way, the right words you choose to think daily are like the riverbank—they give direction to your life. You can look at the river itself as your life story and the riverbank as the words you use to direct that story. If you don't put on words that keep you *aspiring* forward, you will stop flowing freely, becoming stagnant.

I love these words from the book *Letting Go* by Melody Beattie; they express perfectly how we can stay headed in the right direction, flowing freely, as we aspire to grow and change even amid difficulty: "What a journey! This process of growth and change takes us along an ever-changing road. Sometimes the way is hard and craggy. Sometimes we climb mountains. Sometimes we slide down the other side of a toboggan. Sometimes we rest. Sometimes we grope through the darkness. Sometimes we're blinded by sunlight. At times many may walk with us on the road; sometimes, we feel nearly alone. Ever changing, always interesting, always leading someplace better, someplace good." Just reading these words offers me hope and a desire to *aspire*, one step at a time, one day at a time, one word at a time. I hope they will do the same for you, leading and directing you as "word compasses" and "riverbanks" toward all that is good and right for you.

Aspire Together

Another way to *aspire* to your highest potential is to link arms with others and move forward together. The only way to aspire with others is to focus on what you have in common instead of what differentiates you. I often find my inspiration, help, and support through those willing to share their story with me. Over time I have recognized the beauty in others through my relationships with my husband, children, and female friends, even those who seem to be so different from me (like my friend Jody). It has allowed me to fully comprehend that we are not intended to aspire alone. Life is better with a loving family, supportive friends, and wise coaches and mentors. As we reach for desires, recognize our own value, and embrace whom we are meant to be, we can ditch competition and instead focus on connection.

The world is so caught up in the old "Zero Sum" game, which screams at us that we must compete with others for our fair share of the pie (which the petty and greedy claim is not big enough to go around in the first place). Society would have us believe that there is not enough goodness for all of us. But this is a lie. When we work together with others in family, work, and personal relationships, we see there is always enough goodness to go around—or what social behaviorists call Infinite Gain. The more we share, the more we get. The more we connect, the more we create.

It has been my experience that women, in particular, need each other—it doesn't matter our age—for good mental and even physical health (a 2011 *Health* article, "Will You Live to 100?" backs this up, noting that women who have good social connections with other women can add at least five years onto their life expectancy!). We are meant to connect to each other, to support, love, and listen to each other. There is power in sharing our dreams, hopes, and aspirations. I love what Marjorie Pay Hinckley has said about this: "We are all in this together. We need each other. Oh, how we need each other. Those of us who are old need you who are young, and hopefully, you who are young need some of us who are old." Competition isolates us, while community inspires us to cultivate deep, satisfying, and loyal relationships that help us all move toward eternal gain, toward infinite progress.

As I mentioned in the last chapter, I saw the significance of our need to aspire together and decided to organize a gathering of women that was initially called "Certain Women." This group is now called the "Gathering Retreat," and here, women come together with a common purpose—to become aware and awakened to the power of words. During the retreat, we celebrate, connect, and create with words and wisdom.

On the first retreat I hosted, I met a woman named Lory. I was there to teach and mentor her about words, yet what she shared one day about her amazing mother guided me to become better. With Lory's gracious permission, I have included her mother's story:

> I had watched my mom fight an aggressive form of non-Hodgkin's lymphoma for nearly seven years. The cancer spread from her lymph nodes, to her bones, to her lungs, and finally her brain. Years of chemotherapy, radiation, and hospital visits had taken their toll not only on

her body but on our family and our spirits. We stood by helplessly while she endured procedures that brought excruciating pain and suffering with them, all in the name of treatment.

One thing that always impressed me about my mom was that every single time a nurse or doctor came into her room, she thanked them. It didn't matter if they were drawing blood or bone marrow, she thanked them. I was in awe of her gratitude and love for the people around her that were working on her.

When the disease finally settled into her brain, specialists suggested all the options—laser treatment, experimental drugs, surgery. She was willing to try them all, and did.

Surgery was the final option. It would take weeks for the results to come in and a prognosis to be made. My dad and I attended this post-op appointment with my mom. The three of us waited anxiously for the doctor to enter the cold, sterile room with the news. We sat in silence, each of us dealing with the emotions of what the results of the surgery would mean. As the physician stepped into the room, it was apparent that he didn't have good news to share. He sat down, rubbed his forehead, and with sadness in his voice said, "Kathy, I'm so sorry, we've done all we could do, and it just didn't work."

Silence filled the room. My mind spun. My dad began to softly cry. My mom sat still.

Imagine this heartbreaking blow.

Absolute devastation.

A death sentence.

The final word.

My mother, in all her grace and beauty, and with complete sincerity and love, reached over and placed her hand on the doctor's hand and said, "You have the hardest job today. I bet you had no idea how hard today was going to be when you left home this morning. Thank you for being here with me through this."

I was in complete shock and absolute awe of my mother! She was just given a death sentence, and yet she thought about how hard this day was for him? She thought about his two little girls at home and his wife and how the morning must have gone. She thought about his heart and how hard it was for him to come into that room with this kind of news.

I realized my mother was totally empathetic to his situation [and] the hardship of his position, and she had a sincere appreciation and love for him as she continued to aspire along her life journey though [his words] were not the words she had desired to hear.

I learned a lesson that day and am so grateful and appreciative of the words my mom shared and her actions that taught a beautiful lesson of life, a lesson that has left a lasting impression on me.

Whenever I become confused or lose sight of my purpose, it is often words like these Lory shared about her mother that help redirect me to who I am to become. When I get stuck and feel unworthy, I can redirect my mind by putting on the right words, *aspiring* to the greatness within me, to be all that I can no matter where I am in life, just as Lory's exquisite mother was able to do to the very end of her life.

Aspiring through Small, Consistent Steps

Because I love words and the alliteration of words, I asked myself one day what one word I would use to sum up my experiences with putting on words to walk away from my distracted discontent and aspire to a better life. The word *try* came to me as quickly as I asked myself this question. I wrote out the letters, and as soon as I did, I knew what each letter meant to me. T: Today. R: Redirect. Y: Your Thoughts for Good.

T.R.Y. has become my go-to acronym, representing everything the Word Effect does in my life day by day—allowing me to *aspire* onward by consistently taking small and simple steps. Redirecting my thoughts for good by putting on Power Words each day reminds me to stay present, thinking about (and thus feeling) all the good that surrounds me despite the uncertainty of life. *Aspiring* allows me to fail, stumble, and struggle at times while still giving me the courage to move forward consistently.

Microstepping

In 2007, Arianna Huffington, celebrated author, political activist, and co-founder of the *Huffington Post*, collapsed at her desk from extreme exhaustion brought on by overworking herself. She woke up in a pool of blood from a broken cheekbone. In a 2020 Forbes.com article, she shared how that exhaustion led to her decision to leave the *Huffington Post* and launch Thrive Global, a company whose purpose is to help people avoid work and life burnout through a series of "easy-to-adhere-to micro-steps." Thrive Global has a number of corporate clients, including Walmart, but her client base isn't what caught my attention;

it was the "easy-to-adhere-to microsteps" as an approach to changing behavior.

Huffington says, "Behavior change is extremely hard, and we cannot depend on willpower alone. So [Thrive] brought together the power of microsteps . . . steps that we call 'too small to fail,' literally breaking down new behaviors into the smallest possible components and beginning to build a success muscle around them." I love the idea of taking tiny steps because I can do that! I can accomplish a little at a time! That kind of progress feels possible.

My experience with trying to take these "microsteps" in the way I changed the words I was using to describe my life didn't happen overnight. It started with my own research and progressed through ups and downs of failure and triumph each tiny step of the way. I took one word at a time and put it on throughout my day to see how it would change my thinking and perspective. Then I built entire narratives around those words, a little at a time, just as Huffington describes.

Each of the chapters in this book is a little snapshot of the beliefs I told myself over and over to apply, relate to, and associate with each Power Word more deeply. Eventually those beliefs took hold in my life, one consistent action at a time, making it easier to T.R.Y. All this led me to *aspire*, inspiring my imagination with all the possibility and creativity I needed to create a life I now love.

My progress and growth have come from the simple words I have *consistently* chosen to put on each day. I think constancy is the key here—as Huffington makes clear, behavioral change takes time, and success isn't instantaneous. In fact, she is pretty open about the fact that failure was a big part of getting to where she is today. "My life after 2007 was by no means just a series of successes. There were plenty of failures along the way. And I say that . . . because I feel that once people succeed, people bury their failures. And I think it's important for successful people to talk about their failures because it encourages others to take risks."

She also brings up some powerful words her mother used to say to her: "Failure is not the opposite of success, it's a steppingstone to success." In these words lies the truth: accepting defeat along with victory and consistently *aspiring* to do better is simply how we reach our highest potential.

As I have continued to T.R.Y. each day using words to redirect my thoughts and feelings toward my greatest desires, I have been able to move forward even when things don't go as planned. That's because good words produce good thoughts, which produce good feelings, which produce good behaviors. Those good behaviors include being less likely to backslide and get discouraged when times get tough because consistent behavior strengthens the "success muscles" Huffington referred to, making us more resilient and better able to cope with difficulty.

If you want to have the strength to *aspire* to better things, you must be willing to commit to taking small and simple steps—microsteps— to stick with something consistently until you build up the strength in your very soul that will allow you to keep moving forward, keep choosing good, and continuing on your path toward becoming your most beautiful self. I encourage you to apply the T.R.Y. acronym to your own life and see your failures as a necessary part of progressing forward. As you do, you will be able to more consistently grow and aspire.

I will never forget a walk I took one late spring evening a few years back. I was considering a book I desired to write and knew it would be about words when I heard a voice in my mind say, "Notice the steps you have taken to move forward . . . Consider writing about them." As I continued to walk, the seven Power Words began to emerge in my thoughts. I saw the words I had been using to take each step of my journey needed to create a better life.

These steps and words I had been using over and over again acted as a blueprint to change my own approach to life, and I needed to share them with others. I realized I also needed to share the cyclical nature of the Word Effect. Once you go around that circle and aspire to something better, there will be new challenges, new questions, new desires, new dreams, new relationships. The cycle will start all over again, and as you successfully apply the seven Power Words again, you will consistently progress ever forward and upward.

Trust the Aspiring Process

As I explained in the Introduction, when my husband and I were bringing our little ones into the world, I had a difficult time *aspiring* to God's plan because it wasn't *my* plan. Our first child was a boy, and I was fine with that. "What a great way to start our family," I thought, "with a big brother." The second one came shortly after and again was a boy. "Okay," I reasoned. "This is great . . . They will be best friends growing up." But when our third boy came along, all I could think was, "This is *not* the plan!" I like even numbers and I wanted four kids, two boys and two girls. A third boy foiled that plan!

This child, however, turned out to be an absolute delight and brought great joy to our family, so with time I was okay with the fact that he wasn't a girl. When I became pregnant with our fourth baby, I still held out hope for having a girl so we could finally complete our family. Surely this time God would send me the much-wanted daughter whom I deserved! When He didn't give her to me, I was completely bewildered by this supposed injustice.

Although I was pretty heartbroken, I got over it, as I've already confessed previously. Though it took me much longer than it should have, I realized that I had to look at life differently and focus on the amazing gift it is to be a mom of all boys. For those who have all boys, you know what I am talking about. Of course, I've had to grieve things I will miss out on by not having a daughter, and I have worried in the past that all my sons would grow up and forget about me—the old saying, "A daughter's a daughter all her life, but a son's only a son till he gets him a wife," constantly running through my mind.

I would find myself thinking things like "They are sure to grow up and get married and just want to be with their wife's family." But this kind of thinking was simply my attempt at trying to control outcomes over which I had no say. I was spending all my time fretting over the unknowns, unable to trust the process, forgetting to just live in today and find joy now. As I raised my kids, I learned to just take things one day at a time.

After four years of feeling like our family was complete—because let's be frank, four boys are just about enough—my husband and I had individual and personal experiences that made it clear to us there was one more child who was to come to our home. I was thirty-four at the time and had long thought my child-bearing years were over because as I said before, I like even numbers, and a fifth child was not part of the plan. So, when Kris came to me with his impressions, I wasn't open to them at all! "No way!" I told him.

About nine months after my husband told me he thought we should have another baby, I received my own promptings from God that our family was not yet complete. It is something I will never forget. As I was worshipping one day at church, in my mind's eye I saw a baby boy gazing at me; his eyes spoke to me as if to say, "Please don't forget about me." I knew at that moment there was another son who belonged to our family. I guess God has a sense of humor, because He was testing whether I would not only accept His plan to have a fifth child (not an even number!) but also accept that again, it would be a boy.

By this time I had begun to soften my stance on "dictating my plans" to God and instead was *aspiring* daily to follow His plan and His will. "It's high time to accept things just the way they are Becky, to 'be where you are,'" I told myself. So, my husband and I moved forward to bring Jack into this world. Every time I would doubt and panic and wonder "What are we doing?" I was reassured by the beautiful spiritual experience of seeing my fifth son and remembering his words, "Please don't forget about me." That allowed me to be filled with love rather than fear and to trust God (and the process) over myself.

Jack finally arrived five years after our fourth boy. By then we had been out of the "baby on board" stage for a while, and it seemed almost crazy that we were taking this step again. But this step was the one we were supposed to take, designed especially for our family. Jack has been one of the greatest gifts that have come into our lives. He has completed our family in such a way that I thank God every day that He loved us enough to send us this amazing child.

I often wonder what would have happened if I didn't act on the prompting to have another baby and to aspire to God's plan for my family. I really don't know the answer, but I'm just grateful I took the step to align my will with His plan for me—to trust the process.

Think now about how well you are willing to trust the process of becoming. Are you dead set on your own set of plans, like I was? Are you trying to dictate to your higher power or the universe how all things in your life are going to be? Are you filled with a need to control, coerce, or finagle things to fit into a mold you have created for the way life "should" go?

If so, it's likely that even though you may desire to make changes, stop being negative and discontent, see things from a more hopeful perspective, and aspire to a better life, you're not making much progress. Sometimes the best way to start making change is to let go and just sit back into things as you apply the Power Words. Then, as we have already covered in this chapter, venture forth when you are ready and take tiny, manageable microsteps forward. When you do this, you are trusting the process. When you aren't, you are kicking against it, resisting the peaceful, easy flow of the way life unfolds naturally.

The process of growing seeds is an excellent example of how the Earth trusts the cyclical process of becoming and aspires to fulfill the measure of its creation. If you want to grow a garden and have never done it before, you can search the internet for "how to plant seeds," which I did. I share here the first suggestions that came up:

1. Choose a container.
2. Start with quality soil.
3. Plant at the proper depth.

4. Water wisely.
5. Maintain consistent moisture.
6. Keep soil warm.
7. Fertilize.
8. Give seedlings enough light.
9. Circulate the air.
10. Harden off seedlings before transplanting outdoors.

Now unless you have had a little experience with planting seeds, you will need to do a bit more research to fully understand how to accomplish each step on the list. And even with the instructions, things may not go as planned. And nowhere does this internet article remind you that planting seeds and growing takes time; it's simply something you cannot rush. Each spring the ground gets ready for planting, and each fall the harvest comes. It takes time, patience, and trust in the process. The same applies to changing your words, thoughts, feelings, and finally, your actions.

As you aspire to become your best self, you can take the simple words offered in this book and practice putting them on day by day. You can remind yourself to cultivate the right words and trust the process. As I have noted, the Word Effect is cyclical; it has different phases, just like the moon. The moon waxes to a full circle, then wanes to nothing, yet how many times do you even notice it? Its phases are gradual and just happen; it isn't until you become aware of the moon that you begin to focus your mind on it.

In the same way, each of us experiences cycles where we are either waxing or waning—either cycling forward and upward or backward and downward. Once you recognize this and know and trust the process for moving forward, you will be able to see exactly what word you desire to use that day to help you create a life you can love. Over time, just like seedlings, you will grow an amazing garden of possibilities for yourself. But it all starts by trusting the process.

One of the experiences I had with my son, Trevor, when he had been cast in a community play, illustrates just how important it is for us to trust the process by believing not only in the process itself but in ourselves to carry out our part in it. Trevor was so excited to be in the play. He had attended all the practices, prepared his costume, knew his songs, and learned his choreography. Dress rehearsal day arrived when the entire cast would run through the play as if they were giving a live performance. When I dropped Trevor off and wished him luck, he was excited and seemed confident even though he had never acted in anything before.

When I went back to pick him up a few hours later, I couldn't find him. I looked around and finally saw him in the corner of the room, sobbing. He was no longer the excited and confident thirteen-year-old he had been when I dropped him off. What had changed? I wondered if he had been thinking some disturbing words over the last few hours, words that might be forming thoughts that were determining how he was feeling and acting.

I quietly approached him and asked him what was wrong. I waited for him to wipe his eyes, and then he looked up with uncertainty and said, "I can't do this." I responded with "You can't do what?" I will never forget his look of fear and doubt when he said, "I can't do the play." Trevor no longer believed in himself. As I tried to reassure him that a good night's sleep and a new day would help things feel better, he just looked back down at the ground and continued saying quietly so only I would hear, "I can't," over and over again.

Then the most amazing thing happened. An older boy from the group, one that might not have even known who Trevor was except they were both in a song together, became aware of the situation and took it upon himself to reach out. He tapped Trevor on the shoulder and asked, "Are you nervous?" Trevor quietly responded, "Yes." Then this older boy went on to tell my son how he had felt when he first started acting in plays. He validated what Trevor was feeling. He gave him encouragement and reassured him that the next day would be amazing. He then told Trevor, "You *can* do this!" He shared how his experience with dress rehearsals was always a bit hard and often full of nervous jitters, letting Trevor know that this was normal. He reassured my son that all the practice and work would pay off in the end.

This young man's words that night helped Trevor go from feeling very uncertain back to feeling curious and courageous. He helped my son realize that he had prepared himself well for the part and that he could trust the process because of that preparation, redirecting his mind so he could aspire to achieve his goal of acting in community theater. Trevor was able to let things unfold beautifully and fearlessly on opening night.

Just like my son, who had to go to practice consistently to learn the lines, the music, and the dances, we, too, are all part of our own play. We must "go to practice" each day as we journey through life, trusting that as we do, we *can* succeed. When it is time to perform and the nerves set in, we choose to trust the process by choosing the words to help us regain perspective.

A Simple Solution

Consider this simple and doable approach to *aspiring*: you can become your very best by changing one word at a time. Using the power of words, you have the opportunity to breathe life back into your story—to grow and expand all your possibilities. You can ditch your fearful, negative, "stuck" feelings and all the willpower you have been trying to exert to change those feelings, and you can rise up and out of them by changing your words instead. As a good friend of mine recently said, "I don't want my fears to *boss* me around anymore!" When *you* become the boss of your story by changing your words (and thus your thoughts and feelings), you can begin to co-create with God your most beautiful life.

The power of words allows me to trust myself again when I make mistakes along the way. I am a Divine Daughter of Heavenly Parents and aspire to move upward daily. The Power Word *aspire* directs my thoughts and feelings forward, which affects the steps I take, writing a new chapter in my story that is becoming more beautiful than the last.

Each chapter in your story is also being written day by day, the details of which are unfolding right before you. What kind of a tale are you writing? You have more power to create an amazing story than you might have realized. Putting on the right words will allow you to be a full participant in your story instead of sitting on the sidelines just wishing, regretting, and worrying about the things you don't have control over. As you practice putting on words that matter, I cannot emphasize enough how much of a positive impact this will have on your life. You will begin to thrive in ways you have never expected. It seems too simple a solution perhaps—it did for me, too, for a long time—yet as I acted on the prompting from God to change my words, that's when everything started to get a whole lot better. My circumstances haven't changed, yet the words I put on have, and I now experience the Word Effect. Now I look back on my life and it sometimes seems almost unrecognizable.

Today I am creating the life I love and have always desired. I want the same for you. Decide now that you truly are going to *desire to aspire* to the best life you can possibly imagine, and then begin creating it by continuing to T.R.Y. daily, taking those consistent microsteps, and using words as a compass to direct your path toward greatness that is in you. Trust the process, believing that the ability to create a life of beauty and possibility already lives within you. Before going on to the Conclusion, I'd like to invite you to complete the following challenge.

Challenge Your Limited Perspective by Aspiring to Live Your Most Beautiful Life

The challenge to *aspire* is quite simple: be good at being you. To do this, I encourage you to make a "Being Good at Being You" list, where you focus on yourself, your dreams, your desires, and your aspirations.

1. Write down five to ten desires you have been thinking about. These could be little things that come up every day or larger aspirations you want to make happen over time. Start the list this way:

   "I desire . . ." _____

   _____

   _____

   _____

   _____

2. With those aspirations in mind, next decide how you want to feel today. Set an intention of how you want to feel, which can help you decide what words to put on: _____

_____

_____

_____

_____

_____

_____

3. Finally, write three to five ways you can trust in your life's process: _____

_____

_____

_____

_____

_____

_____

"The greatest danger for most of us is not that our aim is too high and we miss it, but that it is too low and we reach it."
—Michelangelo

THE WORD EFFECT'S NEVER-ENDING CYCLE OF JOYFUL LIVING

"The joy we feel has little to do with the circumstances of our lives and everything to do with the focus of our lives."
—Russell M. Nelson

On my family's beloved vacations to Lake Powell, a boating and recreational area on the Utah-Arizona border, my family gets to enjoy nature's beauty as well as fishing, surfing, and relaxing away from the hustle of life. While the trip itself is wonderful, getting ready for and returning from it requires *a lot* of work. Because we stay on a houseboat, we must bring all our needed food for the week, shopping beforehand and even making some of the meals in advance. Other preparations include getting all the equipment and recreational gear ready and making sure everyone has enough clothes. This preparation requires quite a bit of effort and organization.

After the long drive to the dock, we must unload all our clothes, food, and gear onto the houseboat. The houseboat requires some effort to organize and make as enjoyable as possible. We then live in close quarters with a few other families and must help clean up after each meal, keep living spaces picked up, and so forth. In addition to all the living accommodations that must be considered, we must also deal with motorboats and water toys that often need fixing. The fun is sometimes interspersed with mechanical issues and other unexpected problems for which we frequently have to find solutions. I often marvel at the amount of work required to take this trip!

But even with all this work, Lake Powell is my and my family's happy place. We continue to go because we also experience joy while there. That joy continues afterward as we focus on all the fun, relaxation, and memories. Each time we drive home, we reflect on the week and all the good that happened rather than on anything that went wrong.

This makes the effort of getting ready and cleaning up when we return home so worth the trouble because we enjoy so much what we get out of this yearly family excursion.

As we loaded up to head home after one of these joy-filled trips, I said to my husband, "Boy, this vacation to Lake Powell—if we can call it a vacation—sure is a lot of work!" Kris then reminded me that anything of real value takes work. Of course, he is right. Anything of value does require putting in our best effort and never giving up; it is only then that we can find joy in the experience. The memories we have made as a family on these houseboat vacations are priceless and worth all the little steps to get there.

As you know by now, words were my weakness, and because of the words I used to think about my life, I had become very negative and discontent. But God showed me the way to change all this when He inspired me to "change my words." Through making consistent efforts, taking small and simple steps (much like my family and I must do to get ready for these trips to Lake Powell), and seeking God's help, I have discovered how to create a life I love. By *consistently* putting on the seven simple Power Words I have shared with you in this book, my weakness has now become my strength! The words I use to think about my situation and circumstances serve as my compass and allow me to move forward along a fulfilling life path—one that brings me great joy!

I'm so grateful that I can look back and see that Becky, who was filled with discouragement, discontent, and despair, has been transformed into a woman of hopeful, contented joy. This change has only been possible because I was willing to be curious about what God meant when He told me to change my words. I believe that the Almighty gives all of us the gift of curiosity. Just as He did with me, He expects you to open this gift, to make the effort to explore all the ways you can become your best self. God will not force you to do anything or be anyone. It's up to you to choose, using free will, what you want to accomplish and whom you want to become, which is only possible as you remain willing to put in the effort to do so.

I have opened the gift of curiosity and used that gift to explore how words can be used to heal me and jump-start the creative process. That gift has allowed me to move forward, make changes, grow, and become joyful! While this journey has been amazing for me, my heart desires now that you receive this gift as well. As much as I know I was made for joy; I believe you are too.

As I look back at my journey over the last several years, I am amazed at how far I have traveled. I have tried to decide *when* I got to where I am today, but I can see only *how* I made that journey—through the small, simple, consistent steps I took by changing my words. These "microsteps" helped me form solid habits that keep me moving forward. How wonderful it is to see that I am exactly where I need to be because I have chosen to pay attention to the words I use to form my thoughts so I can experience positive feelings and thus create a life filled with beauty and peace. I have shown up for my own story and am living in the present moment, something I'm so grateful I am able to do.

If you haven't shown up yet—to be present in your own story—or feel stuck writing chapters in your life that are taking you nowhere, it's time to make the decision to change the words you are using to write that story. It is time to step into the light and become the person you are meant to be! It is time to open the gift of curiosity and see how the power of words can move you out of a state of suffering and into a beautiful state of becoming.

Trust the Process

In looking back on my journey, I see that I have traveled much like a tortoise must travel. I knew the direction I wanted to go, yet I moved so slowly at times and kept getting distracted, veering off my intended path that I wasn't always sure I was making any improvement. Progress seemed slow and took consistent effort—it still does. But it is these focused, determined attempts, even if they seem to take much longer than anticipated, that have made all the difference.

Of course, the road I have traveled to become has felt scary at times, as I'm sure it will for you as well. There are so many unknowns, so many things we don't plan on. Think about what a tortoise does when it feels threatened: it pulls inside itself and uses its outer shell to protect itself. How often do you pull in on yourself when life gets scary? When things are uncertain, you have every reason to protect yourself by drawing back until you are ready to walk forward again. I have realized it's okay to pause for a time, to take a breath, to be still, to wait. I also know that to live a joyful life, you can't stay still in one place for too long. You must continue moving forward with the dreams and desires of your heart, and the best way to do this is by applying the seven Power Words I have offered in this book. Doing so will allow you to feel curious again—to peek your head out of your shell and, when ready, step forward and move upward as you aspire to become all you are meant to be.

Never Give Up

In addition to trusting the process, getting curious, and peeking your way out of your shell, another important part of becoming requires that you never quit trying. The word "Conclusion" at the beginning of this chapter sounds like you and I might be done with this process . . . but we are not. Continue becoming day by day and recognize your "progress" over "perfection." There are no parameters for how long the journey to becoming your best self might take. No one is dictating to you how fast you must go, not even God Himself. The idea is that you *just keep going*—that every day you T.R.Y. (Today, Redirect Your Thoughts for Good.) It is the consistent efforts to move forward daily that will make all the difference in the long run. The Word Effect is your compass and directs you throughout any and all situations if you allow it to work for you.

When I get a little down about how much time all this becoming can take, I like to think about the pattern of the daily sunrise. It is a consistent pattern, one that we use to plan our day (even though there have been a few days when I have wondered if the sun will even come up at all!). We all live our lives trusting the light will be there every day. The sunrise shows up . . . always. Some days it appears in a sky that is overcast and darker than normal, but it still comes up. It is a gift. I love the simple words my sister-in-law displays on her front door: "Here comes the sun!" These words sound so hopeful because they represent a simple truth in each of our lives: every day you wake up, you have been given another twenty-four hours to take a step or two of progression, try again, and do better. As we head out on our journey, we can take hope that the sun is there to lead and direct us. And if it doesn't seem to be there, we know it will soon be coming. This is a sure thing we count on even if we don't consciously think about it. The Word Effect follows this same pattern. It is another tool to let light into your heart so you can see more clearly the path you are to walk, even if only the next step in front of you. No matter how long the road is, it is a sure thing you can count on.

The seven Power Words of the Word Effect cycle have allowed me to experience my life in a joyful, expansive way; better express my desires and reach for them; and continually work toward becoming my truest and best self. These words, just like the sun, are always there; they can always be counted on. Because we use these words so casually and so frequently, we might not even realize how much of an effect they can have on our lives—much like the sun. But I'm here to tell you, these words have a much more profound impact on us than we know. Their power is there even if we don't stop to see it or have forgotten about it.

One of the patterns that has efficacy in my life, besides how I use words to redirect my thoughts and feelings, is found in my early morning walks. There is a specific design required to go on such a walk. I can't get to the end of the walk until I set out to walk in the first place, so taking that first step is critical (as many have said, the first step is the hardest). But continuing that pattern of putting one foot in front of the other is pivotal. There are no shortcuts in life. Granted, we often try to take them, but these so-called "shortcuts" are mere phantoms. We get where we need to go, we become who we need to be, by going *through* the process, not by trying to bypass it. Time and consistent, focused steps are what accomplish the task. Even though this concept is such a simple one, it is a truth that I did not see immediately in many aspects of my life. Finally, it has now pierced my soul. The key to change of any kind is to start by taking that first step and then con-tinuing to move forward with persistence.

Joyful Living

Of course, the point of all this effort is to change, to grow, to aspire . . . to become! When we are in a state of transformation where we are becoming our truest and best selves, we are also living in a state of pure joy. The Power Words I have learned and shared with you herein have given me the courage, capacity, and commitment needed to take difficult beginning steps and then stay on my designated path so I can experience this joyful living in the present. These words have helped me step out of anxiety and depression and into light and hope, goodness and peace, and a present, joyful life. I have learned how to redirect my mind when I am in a suffering state and fall back into curiosity as I move through the Word Effect cycle. I haven't changed much in my life except for the words I choose to describe my thoughts and feelings. When I change my words, I naturally feel differently, and those feelings are what allow me to live a joy-filled life.

Now, just as I am, you are subject to hateful, demoralizing words, which can cause some pretty negative feelings, including anger and frustration. But I urge you to remember that you have power over the kinds of words you choose to dwell upon. Rather than letting such words, thoughts, and feelings set up residency in your heart, you can choose to think hopeful, encouraging words that can redirect your thoughts for good. Ironically, we must suffer sometimes in order to experience this joy. The president of Brigham Young University, Kevin J. Worthen, has said this regarding joy and suffering: "We should recognize and remember that enduring—constant joy—does not mean uninterrupted bliss and a life free of challenges. Suffering and adversity are part of the eternal plan, a part of the process by which we come to develop enduring joy. Joy helps us transcend temporary trials; it docs not eliminate them from our lives." I know deep in my heart that although sorrow is essential to understanding and experiencing joy, I was not made simply to suffer. I was also made for joy. You were made for joy too.

Think about how you feel after several days of rain when you finally see the beautiful blue sky again. It is almost like you have forgotten how wonderful it is. I live in Utah, where there are, on average, two hundred and sixty days of clear blue skies and sunshine, which showcases the rugged beauty of the Wasatch Mountains near my home. But in the past, I rarely noticed these mountains.

One day I was driving, heading east, and glanced up for some reason to see the amazing white-capped mountains. I thought, "WOW! Those are beautiful!" It was almost like I had an out-of-body experience while taking in their beauty. Then the thought came to me, "Have these mountains always been right before me? Have I never stopped to really notice them?" The truth of it was yes—I was missing the beauty of life *right before me* because I was so focused on my supposed suffering.

I decided it was time to move on to better things. My story is simple, but I have shared it with you because if you have ever felt so many negative emotions that you can't even see God's grace surrounding you, I want you to be free again. Be free to move forward, have hope, and recognize who you truly are. Applying these Power Words each day, each week, each month and each year is what has allowed me to create a joyful life. I am becoming a "light of the world" (Matthew 5:14) with the *power* of *words*. I'm now on a mission to help others discover the healing and creative power found in words.

While the seven Power Words have been game changers for me, I still must practice applying them daily, and they have not magically cured my anxiety and worry. They are in my life as a reminder of what *I* must do every day to move forward with joy. They are my blueprint to living, my compass leading me to a more joyful existence. How will they now impact you?

Putting on empowering words is a little like trying on a pair of new shoes that you have been admiring for some time. They look great in the box, and then you put them on. They feel different and are a bit stiff, and you wonder if you even like them. You must be patient as you break them in and get used to them. Over time the newness of these shoes will wear off, and you will love putting them on—they will become your favorite shoes to wear. These Power Words, possibly unfamiliar to you at first, might feel a little uncomfortable and stiff, like putting on a new pair of shoes. But give these words a try and see what happens. Break them in and continue to practice "wearing" them. You have nothing to lose, and they might just change your entire life as they have mine.

Join me now and discover the *power* of *words*. Awaken your own powerful potential. Move forward one step at a time, one word at a time, with The Word Effect. Remember, you were made for joy! Bring that joy more fully into your life by changing your words so you can change your thoughts, change your feelings, become the person you are meant to be, and live a joyful life full of beautiful possibilities!

www.becomingwithbecky.com

NOTES

INTRODUCTION

Kevin Hall, *Aspire*, (New York: Bookwise Publishing, 2009), "One word could change the world for the better. Words are like passwords. They unlock the power. They open the door."

Brook Castillo, *The Life Coach School Certification Curriculum*, (Austin, Texas: The Life Coach School, 2020), p. 27. "Facts don't hurt. The circumstances of our lives have no effect on us until they encounter the mind and we attach meaning to them."

Kevin Hall, *Aspire*, p. IX; quote taken from the Foreword by Stephen R. Covey. "Words are, and always have been, the creative force of the universe. . . . Used correctly and positively, words are the first building blocks for success and inner peace; they provide the vision and focus that show the way to growth and contribution. Used incorrectly and negatively, they are capable of undermining even the best of intentions. This is true in business, in personal relationships, and in every other walk of life."

Darren Hardy, *The Compound Effect*, (Boston: Da Capo Press, 2010), p. 3; quoting Jim Rohn. "There are no new fundamentals. Truth is not new—it is old."

CHAPTER 1

Ann Voskamp, *www.annvoskamp.com*. "You can spend the time distressed, discontent, distracted, discouraged, dissatisfied or you can spend the time enjoying, engaging, enriched. The only decision you have to make today is what you 'do with your time.'"

Harry S. Truman, *www.brainyquote.com*. "A pessimist is one who makes difficulties of his opportunities and an optimist is one who makes opportunities of his difficulties."

Paul Rozin and Edward B. Royzman, "Negativity Bias, Negativity Dominance, and Contagion," *Personality and Social Psychology Review*, (2001), p. 296. "There is a general bias, based on both innate predispositions and experience, in animals and humans, to give greater weight to negative entities (e.g., events, objects, personal traits)."

Kendra Cherry, "What Is the Negativity Bias?" (*https://www. verywellmind.com/negative-bias-4589618#toc-what-is-the-negativity-bias*), April 29, 2020. "Have you ever found yourself dwelling on an insult or fixating on your mistakes? Criticisms often have a greater impact than compliments and bad news frequently draws more attention than good. The reason for this is the negative events have a greater impact on our brains than positive ones. Psychologists refer to this as the negative bias, or negativity bias, and it can have a powerful effect on your behavior, your decisions, and even your relationships."

Margaret Jaworski, "The Negativity Bias: Why the Bad Stuff Sticks," *Remedy Health Media* (www.psycom.net), February 2020. "Not only do negative events and experiences import more quickly, but they also linger longer than positive ones. The negativity bias can even cause you to dwell on something negative even if something positive is equally or more present."

Kendra Cherry, "What Is the Negativity Bias?" (*www.verywellmind. com*). "In most interactions, we are more likely to notice negative things and later remember them more vividly. This bias toward the negative leads you to pay much more attention to the bad things that happen, making them seem much more important than they really are."

Brook Castillo, *The Life Coach School Certification Curriculum*, (Austin, Texas: The Life Coach School, 2021), p. 92. "Emotional childhood occurs when grown adults have not matured past childhood in terms of managing their emotions. This means they react to their emotions, act out, or avoid emotions rather than taking full responsibility and choosing thoughts that will create more desirable and appropriate emotions. In short, emotional childhood is not taking responsibility for how you feel."

Nielsen, Norman Group, "The Negativity Bias in User Experience," (*www.nngroup.com*), October 23, 2016 "Imagine you went on a beautiful hike and along the trail you encountered a rattlesnake. What do you think you will remember more vividly about the hike: the snake you encountered or the beautiful scenery along the way? Most people . . ."

Brooke Castillo, *How to Have A Better Life: Tools from a Master Life Coach*, (Austin, Texas: The Life Coach School, 2020), pg 64. "We are in charge of how we think, we are in charge of how we feel. When we are functioning as emotional children, we are blaming other people [or circumstances] for how we feel, how we act, and for the results we get in our life."

TLEX Institute, "Mind Matters: How to Effortlessly Have More Positive Thoughts," (*https://tlexinstitute.com/how-to-effortlessly-have-more-positive-thoughts/*). "We can see that one of the tendencies of the mind is to focus on the negative and 'play the same songs' over and over again."

Ibid. "[Of] the 15 percent of the worries that did happen, 79 percent of the subjects discovered that either they could handle the difficulty better than expected, or that the difficultly taught them a lesson worth learning. The conclusion is that 97 percent of our worries are baseless and result from an unfounded pessimistic perception."

Kevin Hall, *Aspire*, p. IX; from the Foreword by Stephen R. Covey. "Used correctly, and positively, words are the first building blocks for success and inner peace; they provide the vision and focus that show the way to growth and contribution . Used incorrectly, and negatively, they are capable of undermining even the best of intentions. This is true in business, in personal relationships, and in every other walk of life."

Brooke Castillo, *Self Coaching Scholars Curriculum Workbook*, (Austin, Texas: The Life Coach School, 2021), p. 4. "Decisions are the ultimate power we have in our lives! A simple decision is simply a commitment to a thought, feeling and action that creates a result."

CHAPTER 2

Alex Blackwell, *www.quotefancy.com*. "The first step on the path to positive change is acknowledgement that change is necessary and possible. Open yourself to the possibility of seeing the world in a new way. What do you have to lose?"

Brené Brown, *The Gifts of Imperfection*, (Center City, Minnesota: Hazelden, 2010). "Perfectionism . . . fuels this primary thought: If I look perfect, and do everything perfectly, I can avoid or minimize the painful feelings of shame, judgment, and blame."

Brené Brown, "The Power of Vulnerability," TED Talk presented in Houston, Texas, June 2010. "We live in vulnerable world and we numb vulnerability. We are the most in debt, obese, addicted, and medicated adult cohort in U.S. history. . . . The problem is you cannot selectively numb emotion. You can't say, 'Here's the bad stuff. Here is vulnerability, shame, fear, disappointment. I don't want to feel these. . . .' When we numb those, we numb joy, gratitude, and happiness [as well] and then we feel miserable."

Brené Brown, *The Gifts of Imperfection*. "Perfectionism, after all, is an ultimately self-defeating way to move through the world. It is built on an excruciating irony— making, and admitting mistakes is a necessary part of growing and learning and being human. . . . By avoiding mistakes at any cost, a perfectionist can make it harder to reach their own lofty goals."[3]

Anne Wilson Schaef, (*www.goodreads.com*). "Perfectionism is self-abuse of the highest order."

Elizabeth Gilbert, *Big Magic: Creative Living beyond Fear*, (London: Penguin Publishing Group, 2016). "Perfection is unachievable: It's a myth and a trap and a hamster wheel that will run you to death."

Brené Brown, *The Gifts of Imperfection*. "Perfectionism is not to be confused with healthy striving, which is self-focused [and asks] 'how can I improve?'"

Brooke Castillo, *Self Coaching Six Week Program*, (Austin, Texas: The Life Coach School, 2021), p. 21. "Just like a fish is unaware of the water in which it swims, we are often unaware of the thoughts we're thinking. We must develop the skill of becoming a 'Watcher' [over] our thoughts. We have to learn to watch our brain think so we can recognize thoughts and beliefs for what they are."

Marie Forelo, *Everything Is Figureoutable*, (New York: Portfolio/ Penguin Random House, 2019), p. 7. "There can be no significant change in the world unless we first have the courage to change ourselves. In order to change ourselves, we must first believe we can."

Craig Manning, *The Fearless Mind*, (Springville, Utah: Cedar Fort, 2009), pp. 55–56. "I'm from Australia, and crocodiles are aggressive creatures. They will take us even when they are not hungry. . . . "My professor . . . [then] asked me to visualize being in a room with no way out except for one door. He [asked me] to visualize a croc coming around the corner . . ."

Christine Lavulo, *Women Who Empower*, (www.katebutler.com: Kate Butler Books, 2020), p. 233.

"I was working with a business coach to get my speaking and coaching going, and she took me through some exercises so we could narrow down my core theme. We talked about words [and those] that express who I am and the experiences that qualify me for this particular career. It came down to one word . . . overcomer. I have overcome many . . ."

JP Sears, "How to Be More Afraid," *AwakenWithJP*, (https://m.youtube.com/watch?v=IcX9HBG4L34), July, 2020. "To learn how to be more afraid, always choose a feeling of safety over a feeling of aliveness. Instead of asking the person out, taking the adventure, leaving the job you hate, or doing the thing you've never done before, avoid those dangers so you can keep the pacifier of safety in your mouth . . . because that feels better!"

Brook Castillo, *The Life Coach School Certification Curriculum*, p. 94. "Somewhere, typically in our early adulthood, we stop focusing on our future and focus instead on our past to help us decide what we're capable of. We begin choosing thoughts like, 'I've never done it before so I'm not sure I can do it,' 'I've always been overweight; it's just who I am,' or 'I've never been . . .'"

Walt Whitman, *www.goodreads.com*. "Not I, not anyone else can travel that road for you, you must travel it for yourself."

CHAPTER 3

Suzy Kassem, *Rise Up and Salute the Sun: The Writings of Suzy Kassem*, (www.goodreads.com). "To seek truth requires one to ask the right questions. Those void of truth never ask about anything because their ego and arrogance prevent them from doing so. Therefore, they will always remain ignorant. Those on the right path of Truth are extremely heart-driven and childlike . . ."

The Life Coach School, *The Life Coach School Certification Curriculum*, (Austin, Texas: The Life Coach School, 2021), p. 48. "Questions reveal thoughts and can also direct us to think new ones . . . don't ever underestimate how many of us are on auto pilot, playing out the programming of our childhoods without questioning it. We do what we think we should do based on what we were told as children, and we have never evaluated whether it still applies."

Ibid., p. 50: "If you were to ask a client, 'why can't you lose weight?' the person will give you all the reasons why they can't lose weight. Alternatively, when you ask a client a positive question, they'll answer with positive thoughts. For example, 'How have you been successful at this?' Or 'How can you enjoy this process?'"

Ibid. "By asking high quality, empowering questions, we get creative and inspiring answers. It's like our brain goes to work searching for the answers to what we're presenting."

Oliver Wendell Holmes, *The Autocrat of the Breakfast Table* (Boston and New York: Houghton, Mifflin and Company, 1891). "The mind that opens to a new idea never returns to its original size."

The Life Coach School, *Certification Curriculum*, p. 51. "If you ask yourself, 'why can't I lose weight?' you'll come back with a slew of very negative, self-defeating answers. The question incorporates a negative belief and your brain will be sent to task to prove that negative belief correct. Your brain is . . ."

Napoleon Hill, *Think and Grow Rich*, (New York: Penguin, 2004). "Thomas Edison had an extraordinarily positive perception of life that greatly enhanced his ability as an inventor. When others might have been hopelessly discouraged after failing thousands of times in an attempt to develop an electric light, the great Edison simply viewed each unsuccessful experiment as the elimination of a solution that wouldn't work, thereby . . ."

Thomas Edison, (*www.thoughts.com/edison-quotes-1991614*). "I have not failed. I've just found 10,000 ways that won't work. . . . Just because something doesn't do what you planned it to do doesn't mean it's useless."

Richard G. Scott, "For Peace at Home," General Conference of The Church of Jesus Christ of Latter-day Saints, April 2013. "Remember, little things lead to big things. Seemingly insignificant indiscretions or neglect can lead to big problems. More importantly, simple, consistent, good habits lead to a life full of bountiful blessings."

Albert Einstein, *Life Magazine* (May 2, 1955). "The important thing is not to stop questioning. Curiosity has its own reason for existing."

Steve Jobs, (*https://minimalistquotes.com/steve-jobs-quote-12518/*). "Most people never ask, that's what separates the people that do things from the people that just dream about them."

Marie Forleo, *Everything Is Figureoutable*, p. 19. "I felt like a total failure. Less than a year earlier, I'd graduated the valedictorian of Seton Hall University. Yet here I was sitting on the steps of Trinity Church in lower Manhattan, in tears. As a trading assistant on the floor of the New York Stock exchange on Wall Street, I had pride, a steady paycheck, and health insurance. I was grateful . . ."

Ibid., p.20. "For a while, I tried to ignore that small voice inside . . . but the voice only grew louder. Then, one day I was running tickets on the floor of the exchange and started to feel physically sick. I couldn't breathe. I told my boss I needed to head . . ."

Ibid., p. 23. "I stumbled across an article about a brand-new profession, 'coaching' (this was the late 1990s—it was all so new back then) . . . [and] when I read the article . . . something inside me lit up. . . . A deep, gentle presence inside me said, 'This is who you are. This is who you're meant to be.'"

Malcolm Forbes, (*www.quotefancy.com*). "One who never asks either knows everything or nothing."

CHAPTER 4

Jim Rohn, (*www.goodreads.com*). "You must take personal responsibility. You cannot change the circumstances, the seasons, or the wind, but you can change yourself. That is something you have charge of."

Theodore Roosevelt, (*https://www.psychologytoday.com/us/blog/multiple-choice/201903/is-comparison-really-the-thief-joy?amp*). "Comparison is the thief of joy."

Mark Twain, (*www.goodreads.com*). "Comparison is the death of joy."

Eric Bjarnson, *Some Universals, Volume 3: Acceptance and Resistance*, (Little Mountain Publications: Lindon, Utah), 2022. "Acceptance is surrendering resistance to God, self, others, and all aspects of life on earth and opening up your heart to receive all the blessings and learning opportunities the Lord is continually showering down upon you."

George Lucas, (*www.goodreads.com*). "Always remember your focus determines your reality."

Tobias Schneider, "If You Want It You Might Get It—The Reticular Activating System Explained," (*https://medium.com/desk-of-van-schneider/if-you-want-it-you-might-get-it-the-reticular-activating-system-explained-761b6ac14353*), 2017. "The Reticular Activating System (RAS) is a bundle of nerves at our brainstem that filters out unnecessary information, so the important stuff gets through. The RAS is the reason you learn a new word and then start hearing . . ."

HappiMe App, "I Can Do It," (*https://youtube.com/QCnfAzAlhVw*), 2013. "Your RAS acts as a filter against the data that is around you (sounds, tastes, colors, images, pictures). There can be up to 2,000,000 bits of data at any time! Your brain can only process so much at a time. So your RAS filter only lets things through that it thinks are important. So, how does . . ."

Marie Forleo, *Everything Is Figureoutable*, p 53. "You are 100 percent responsible for your life. Always and in all ways, it's not your parents. It's not the economy. It's not your husband, or your wife, or your family. It's not your boss. It's not the schools you went to. It's not the government or society or institution or your age. You are responsible . . ."

Darren Hardy, *The Compound Effect*, p. 9. "The compound effect is the principle of reaping huge rewards from a series of small and smart choices. The changes are so subtle, almost imperceptible."

Brooke Castillo, *The Life Coach School Business Eight Week Program*, (Austin, Texas: The Life Coach School, 2020), p. 40. "A feeling, also an emotion, is a vibration in your body. Nothing more. Without exception, feelings come from our thoughts. They don't 'happen' to us. We create them with our thoughts. . . . Feelings always follow thoughts and never the other way around."

Chad Hymas, *Doing What Must Be Done*, (Rush Valley, Utah: Chad Hymas Communications, 2004), p. 46. "Staring at the stark white composite ceiling . . . I [could] no longer hope to accomplish the dreams that lent enthusiasm and energy to my life."

Ibid., p. 47.

"As thoughts darken my mood, in comes the cavalry to the rescue. I could almost hear bugles and padding hooves. It's Dad. Dad has become my own personal, self-appointed motivational speaker. He begins with gentle enthusiasm, 'Son, I know this seems impossible, but. . . .' I know he's trying to be helpful. I know he is coming from a place of love and he doesn't want . . ."

Ibid., p.49.

"I watched the [speech] without protest. What else am I going to do? I can't even turn my head. When the speech is over, I don't remember one thing Art said. I do now because I've watched it since—many times— and I still watch it every so often to remind myself of how possible impossible is. A few weeks later, my hospital room door suddenly bumps . . ."

Michael J. Fox, (*www.brainyquote.com*). "My happiness grows in direct proportion to my acceptance, and in inverse proportion to my expectations."

University of Hertfordshire, "Self-acceptance Could Be the Key to a Happier Life, Yet It's the Happy Habit Many People Practice the Least," *Science Daily,* (*https://www.sciencedaily.com/releases/2014/03/ 140307111016.html*), 2014; quoting Mark Williamson. "Our society puts huge pressure on us to be successful and to constantly compare ourselves with others. This causes a great deal of unhappiness and anxiety. These findings remind us that if we can learn to be more accepting of ourselves as we really are, we're likely to be much happier. The results also confirm to us that our day-to-day habits have a much bigger impact on our happiness than we might imagine."

Deborah Reber, *Chicken Soup for the Teenage Soul,* (*www.goodreads.com*). "Letting go doesn't mean that you don't care about someone anymore. It's just realizing that the only person you really have control over is yourself."

CHAPTER 5

Wayne Dyer, (*www.brainyquote.com*). "Abundance is not something we acquire. It is something we tune into."

Eckhart Tolle, *A New Earth: Awakening to Your Life's Purpose,* (*www. goodreads.com*). "Acknowledging [and accepting] the good that you already have in life is the foundation for all abundance."

Hazelden Publishing, *Twenty-four Hours a Day,* (Center City, Minnesota: Hazelden Publishing, 1954). "I pray that today I may have inner peace. I pray that today I may be at peace with myself."

Johnson Oatman, Jr., "Count Your Blessings," *Hymns* (The Church of Jesus Christ of Latter-day Saints: Salt Lake City), 1985, No. 241.

Richard Paul Evans, *The Four Doors, A Guide to Joy, Freedom and a Meaningful Life,* (New York: Simon & Schuster, 2013), p. 12. "All creation begins in the mind as a thought or idea. Though all thoughts do not originate within our minds, that which we choose to focus on grows in significance. The power to focus and direct our thoughts . . ."

Ralph Waldo Emerson, (*www.goodreads.com*). "Every revolution was first a thought in one man's mind."

Richard Paul Evans, *The Four Doors,* p. 12. "Individually, the crabs could easily climb out of the pot except that the other crabs will pull down any crab that tries to escape. The analogy to the human condition is obvious. It is a common social phenomenon that members . . ."

Stephen R. Covey, *The Seven Habits of Highly Effective People* (New York: Simon & Schuster, 1989). "Most people are deeply scripted in what I call the Scarcity Mentality. They see life as having only so much, as though there were only one pie out there. And if someone were to get a big piece of the pie, it would mean less for everybody else."

Tony Robbins, (*www.goodreads.com*). "When you are grateful, fear disappears, and abundance appears."

Esther Hicks, (*www.quotefancy.com*). "The fastest way to bring more wonderful examples of abundance into your personal experience is to take constant notice of the wonderful things that are already there."

CHAPTER 6

Martin Luther King, Jr., (*www.goodreads.com*). "Take the first step in faith. You don't have to see the whole staircase, just take the first step."

Babe Ruth, (*www.goodreads.com*). "Never let the fear of striking out keep you from playing the game."

Tony Robbins, (*www.quotefancy.com*). "The only limit to your impact is your imagination and commitment."

Brené Brown, *Dare to Lead: Brave Work. Tough Conversations. Whole Hearts*, (New York: Random House Audio). "Vulnerability is not winning or losing. It's having the courage to show up when you can't control the outcome."

W.H. Murray, *www.goodreads.com*. "Until one is committed there is hesitancy, the chance to draw back, always ineffectiveness. Concerning all acts of initiative (and creation), there is one elementary truth, the ignorance of which kills countless ideas and splendid plans: that the moment one definitely commits oneself, then Providence moves too. All sorts of things occur to help one that would never otherwise..."

J.K. Rowling, (*www.libquotes.com*). "We do not need magic to change the world, we carry all the power we need inside ourselves already: we have the power to imagine better."

James Clear, quoting *Forbes* magazine in "How to Stop Procrastination on Your Goals by Using the 'Seinfeld Strategy,'" (*www.jamesclear.com*). (Jerry Seinfeld's peak earnings in 1998 of $267 million; and in 2008 still pulling in $85 million annually.)

James Clear, "How to Stop Procrastination on Your Goals by Using the 'Seinfeld Strategy,'" (*www.jamesclear.com*). "What is most impressive about Seinfeld's career isn't the awards, the earnings, or the special moments; it's the remarkable consistency of it all. Show after show, year after year, he performs, creates, and entertains at an incredibly high standard. Jerry Seinfeld produces with a level of consistency that most of us wish we could bring to our daily work . . ."

Chloe Britton, "The Seinfeld Effect: Maintaining the Chain to the Brain," (*https://blog.wranx.com/the-Seinfeld-effect-maintaining-the-chain-to-the-brain*). "In Seinfeld's case, [he wrote] a minimum amount of jokes daily. . . . It's all in doing, the achieving. . . . The key is to never break the chain [of doing the little things]. That would leave a gap and mean starting again, and nobody wants to do that."

Darren Hardy, *The Compound Effect*, p. 9. "The Compound Effect is the principle of reaping huge rewards from a series of small, smart choices. What's most interesting about this process to me is that even though the results are massive, the steps, in the moment, don't feel significant. Whether you're using this strategy for improving your health, relationships, finances, or anything else for that matter, the changes are so subtle, they're almost . . ."

Michael Dunn, "One Percent Better," General Conference of The Church of Jesus Christ of Latter-day Saints, October, 2021. "That new approach would reveal an eternal principle—with a promise—regarding our oft times perplexing mortal quest to improve ourselves. . . . Unlike previous coaches who attempted dramatic, overnight turnarounds, Sir Brailsford instead committed to a strategy . . ."

Howard W. Hunter, "What Is True Greatness?" *Great Speeches: Brigham Young University*, (1987). "True greatness . . . always requires regular, consistent, small, and sometime ordinary and mundane steps over a long period of time."

Gordon B. Hinckley, "Be True to the Faith," Brigham Young University devotional address, September 18, 2007. "To be virtuous is to be strong—to have the strength to do whatever needs doing. Great virtue comes in doing *well* and *consistently* the everyday, often rather tedious tasks of life."

Darren Hardy, *The Compound Effect*, p. 10. "Let's say you take the cold, hard cash and your friend goes the penny route. On Day Five, your friend has sixteen cents. You, however, have $3 million. On Day Ten, it's $5.12 versus your big bucks. After 20 full days, with only 11 days left in the month, your friend only has . . ."

Dan Sullivan, *The 4 C's Formula*, (Toronto, Ontario: The Strategic Coach Inc., 2015). "Have you ever wondered why some people are super-achievers and seem to go from success to success while others never seem to get out of the starting blocks? In my 40 years of coaching high-achieving entrepreneurs, I've noticed that they all go through a process to help them break through to the next level of success."

Brooke Castillo, *The Life Coach School Business Eight Week Program*, (Austin, Texas: The Life Coach School), p. 45. "If a goal is worth accomplishing, if a goal stretches us and expands our potential, then we'll feel uncomfortable as we work toward it. So when we look at it this way, discomfort is a sign that we're on the right track. It's a sign that we are growing and expanding, becoming the next best version of ourselves."

Elle Sommer, (*https://me.me/i/every-success-begins-with-a-decision-to-try-and-a-6430628*). "Every success story started with a decision to try and a commitment to keep going."

CHAPTER 7

Margaret Cousins, (*www.goodreads.com*). "Appreciation can make a day, even change a life. Your willingness to put it into words is all that is necessary."

Laurel Dawn Huston, Reflections Inside and Out Mentoring Group coaching call, November 2021. "Appreciation is a feeling of being grateful for something or someone, an ability to understand the worth, quality, or importance of something. Look at the scenario and say, what about this [situation] happened *for* me instead of *to* me?"

Mike Robbins, "The Power of Appreciation," TEDxBellevue speech presented in Bellevue, Washington, November 15, 2013. "I learned about the power of appreciation in a pretty significant way when something pretty important was taken away from me: my professional baseball career."

Ibid. "So just like that, after starting baseball when I was seven, my career ended. Now as you can imagine I was pretty devastated. When the reality of the fact that my baseball career was over finally set in, I started to ask myself over and over again, *did I have any regrets?* And you know . . ."

Ibid. "I was a kid from Oakland, California, raised by a single mom who didn't have a lot of money and always wanted to grow up and make it to the major leagues and be someone important."

Kevin Hall, *Aspire*, p. 98. "It's been said that vision is what we see when we close our eyes. We have to see it before we can be."

Dieter F. Uchtdorf, "Of Things that Matter Most" General Conference of The Church of Jesus Christ of Latter-day Saints, October 2010. "If life and its rushed pace and many stresses have made it difficult for you to feel like rejoicing, then perhaps now is a good time to refocus on what matters most. When stress levels rise, when distress appears, when tragedy strikes, too often we attempt to keep up the same frantic pace or even accelerate, thinking somehow that the more rushed our pace, the better off we will be."

Ibid. "Let's be honest, it's rather easy to be busy. We all can think up a list of tasks that will overwhelm our schedules. Some might even think that their self-worth depends on the length of their to-do list. They flood the open spaces in their time with lists of meetings and minutia—even during times of stress and fatigue. Because they unnecessarily complicate their lives, they often feel increased frustration, diminished joy, and too little sense of meaning in their lives."

John C. Maxwell, (*www.quotefancy.com*). "Life is a matter of choices, and every choice you make makes you."

Pat Forde, "I've Covered Nine Olympics. Nothing Prepared Me for Seeing My Daughter Win a Medal," *Sports Illustrated*, (August 5, 2021). "Moments like that, it's so much fun . . . but moments at [training] camp are where we become Team USA. It's the . . . little moments—it's not the big moments that are caught on camera. It's the moments you don't . . ."

Newel E. Kimball, *The Newel and Gloria Kimball Family*, (Oxbow Publishing: Victor, Idaho, 2020), p. 218. "Apparently, God expects us to accept everything with a sense of thankfulness: for life itself; the eternal nature of the soul and all that pertains to the maintenance, enjoyment, and continuance of it; the beauty surrounding us everywhere; the aromas; the colors; the food; revealed science and technology; travel; animals; people; the senses that perceive . . .”

Hazelden Publishing, *The Twenty-four Hours a Day Book*. “Sunshine is the laughter of nature. Live out in the sunshine. The sun and air are good medicine. Nature is a good nurse for tired bodies. Let her have her way with you. God’s grace is like the sunshine. Let your whole . . .”

Dr. Seuss, (*www.quotepark.com*). “Sometimes you will never know the value of a moment until it becomes a memory.”

Ariana Grande, *www.quotefancy.com*. “Life is beautiful. Cherish every moment even if you are stressed or hurt or whatnot. There’s always a tomorrow and it always gets better.”

CHAPTER 8

Joe Dispenza, (*https://www.icreatedaily.com/dr-joe-dispenza-quotes/*). “Becoming the person you aspire to be requires that you stop being that old self.”

Maya Angelou, (*www.goodreads.com*). Do the best you can until you know better and when you know better, do better.”

Melody Beattie, *The Language of Letting Go*, (Center City, Minnesota: Hazelden Publishing, 1990). “What a journey! This process of growth and change takes us along an ever-changing road. Sometimes the way is hard and craggy. Sometimes we climb mountains. Sometimes we slide down the other side of a toboggan. Sometimes we rest. Sometimes we grope through the darkness . . .”

Stephanie Dolgoff, “Will You Live to 100?,” *Health*, (March 2011), p. 132. (Women who are social can add up to five years to their life expectancy.)

Bonnie L. Oscarson, "Sisterhood: Oh, How We Need Each Other," quoting Marjorie Pay Hinckley in her General Conference address of The Church of Jesus Christ of Latter-day Saints, April 2014. "We are all in this together. We need each other. Oh, how we need each other. Those of us who are old need you who are young, and hopefully, you who are young need some of us who are old."

Steve Forbes, "Microsteps toward Thriving with Arianna Huffington," *Forbes.com*, (January 22, 2021), quoting Arianna Huffington. "Behavior change is extremely hard, and we cannot depend on willpower alone. So [Thrive] brought together the power of microsteps . . ."

Ibid. "My life after 2007 was by no means just a series of successes. There were plenty of failures along the way. And I say that . . . because I feel that once people succeed, people bury their failures. And I think it's important for successful people to talk about their failures, because it encourages others to take risks. . . . Failure is not the opposite of success, it's a stepping stone to success."

Zig Zigler, (*www.brainyquotes.com*). "Gratitude is the healthiest of all human emotions."

Madhuleena Roy Chowdhury, "The Neuroscience of Gratitude and How It Affects Anxiety and Grief," *Positive Psychology.com*, (March 2022). "Anxiety is our body's inbuilt wake-up call that alerts us against danger. When fear sets in, our body releases hormones that create the fight or flight responses, and we react likewise. The brain doesn't get much time to analyze the right or wrong when the adrenaline rush . . ."

Oprah Winfrey, (*www.brainyquote.com*). "Be thankful for what you have, you'll end up having more. If you concentrate on what you don't have, you will never ever have enough."

Michelangelo, (*www.goodreads.com*). "The greatest danger for most of us is not that our aim is too high and we miss it, but that it is too low and we reach it."

CONCLUSION

Russel M. Nelson, "Joy and Spiritual Survival," General Conference of The Church of Jesus Christ of Latter-day Saints, October 2016. "The joy we feel has little to do with the circumstances of our lives and everything to do with the focus of our lives."

Edward Eyestone, "Run Like a Horse," *BYU Magazine*, (Winter 2016), p. 47. "During my freshman year there was one goal that sounded like it would etch my name into athletic immortality: becoming an All-American. . . . I decided I wanted this title my freshman year. I didn't want to wait until I was a senior. To become All-American meant making it to the national [cross-country] meet and then finishing in the top six in your event. . . . That year nationals were in Austin, Texas, where an incredible heat wave . . ."

Thomas Paine, (*www.goodreads.com*). "What we obtain too cheaply, we esteem too lightly; that is valued only which is dear. Heaven knows how to put a proper price on its goods."

Kevin J. Worthen, "Enduring Joy," Brigham Young University devotional address, January 7, 2020. "We should recognize and remember that enduring—constant joy—does not mean uninterrupted bliss and a life free of challenges. Suffering and adversity are part of the eternal plan, a part of the process by which we come to develop enduring joy. Joy helps us transcend temporary trials; it does not eliminate them from our lives."

ABOUT THE AUTHOR

Driven by the desire to spread and inspire goodness, Becky Kemp is dedicated to sharing the power found in positive words. From the onset of her clothing brand, Becoming Threads, to her current podcast, called "The Word Effect," she loves speaking and coaching about how words matter!

Becky is a certified life coach and mentor who is dedicated to helping others recognize that change is possible and that each of us is capable of creating a beautiful life. She also serves as a board member of the National Speaker's Association, Mountain West Chapter and in the National Speakers Association, and is an active volunteer in her church and community.

Becky is married to her high school sweetheart and the mother of five children, and proudly known by her two grandchildren as 'Grandma Becky!' In her free time, she loves quiet early mornings; walking her dog, Marley; boating on Lake Powell with her family; and watching her son still at home play baseball.

For more information on Becky's coaching services and women's retreats or to book her to speak at your next function, visit www.becomingwithbecky.com. Follow Becky on Facebook and Instagram @becomingwithbecky and subscribe to "The Word Effect" podcast on your favorite app to listen to podcasts.